The Korean War

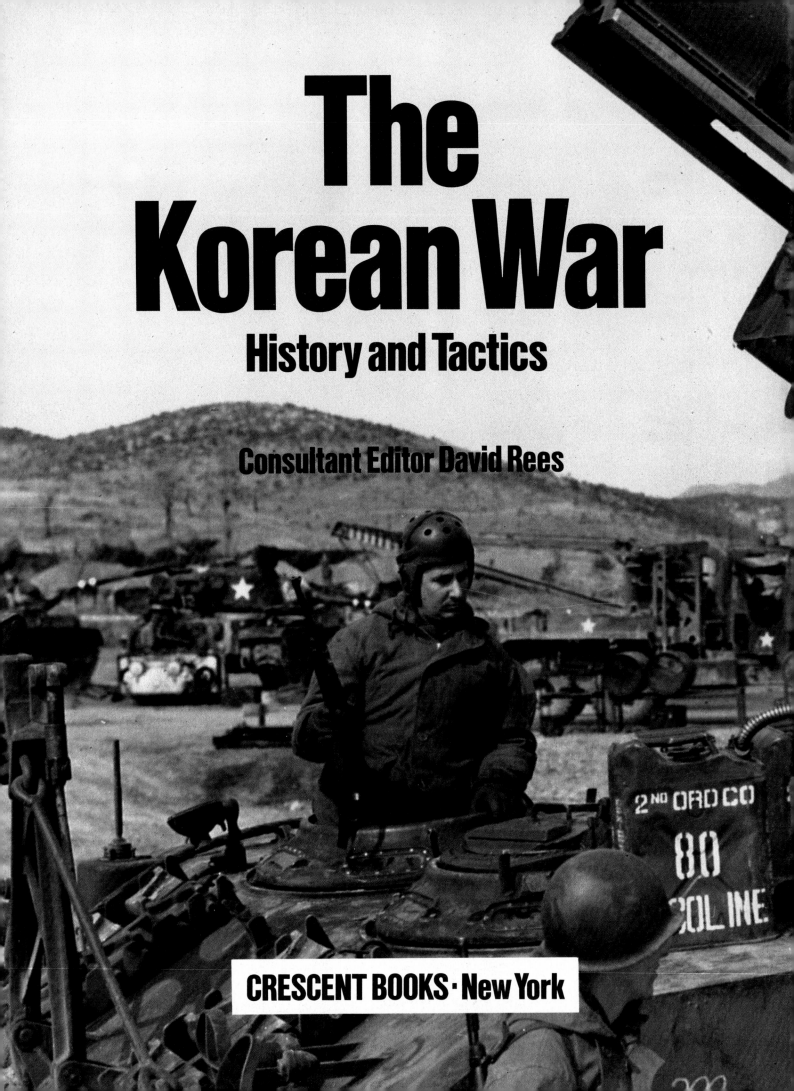

The Korean War

History and Tactics

Consultant Editor David Rees

CRESCENT BOOKS · New York

Consultant editor
David Rees is Senior Research Fellow of the Institute for the Study of
Conflict in London and writes for its publications on international affairs.
He is a well known authority on the Korean War, having written *Korea –
The Limited War*, a standard work on the subject. He is the author of
several other books on twentieth-century history, including a biography
of Harry Dexter White.

The authors
P. J. Banyard is a former member of the British Army who specialises in
the relationship between military history and technology.

Ian Beckett is a senior lecturer in the Department of War Studies and
International Affairs at Sandhurst. He is the co-author of *Politicians and
Defence*.

Major F. A. Godfrey MC served in Malaya, Cyprus, Malta, Libya, Aden
and Berlin before retiring from the British Army in 1969. From 1973 to
1982 he was on the teaching staff of the Royal Military Academy,
Sandhurst.

Bryan Perrett is a military historian with a special interest in modern
armoured warfare. His recent books include *Weapons of the Falklands
Conflict*.

Anthony Robinson is one of Britain's leading experts on military aviation.
Formerly on the staff of the RAF Museum, Hendon, he has edited *Aerial
Warfare* and the aviation encyclopedia *Wings*.

Brigadier-General Edwin H. Simmons, US Marine Corps Retired is Director
of Marine Corps History and Museums. He is widely published, especially
on topics concerning the US Marines, and is the author of the standard
work *The United States Marines*.

Editors Ashley Brown, Richard Williams
Designer Mick Hodson

© 1984 by Orbis Publishing, London

This 1984 edition is published by Crescent Books
Distributed by Crown Publishers Inc.

Printed in Italy

ISBN 0-517-439360

Library of Congress Catalog Card Number: 84-071494

Contents

Introduction and Prelude

The partition of Korea along the 38th parallel in 1945, followed by the intense postwar rivalry between the United States and the Soviet Union, led directly to the Korean War of 1950–53. But Korea's geographical position, set as it is between China, Japan and Russia, had long made it a focus for the rivalries of the great powers in the Far East. Consequently, many of the more important military events of the 1950–53 war were foreshadowed by the conflicts in Korea's turbulent past.

From the Yalu River, the border with Manchuria, the Korean peninsula extends southwards towards the Japanese islands. The peninsula is about 970km (600 miles) long and on average about 240km (150 miles) wide. The total area of the country is about 220,000km² (85,000 sq. miles) and thus Korea is equal in size to Great Britain or New York State. To the south of Korea, the Japanese home island of Honshu lies about 210km (130 miles) from Pusan across the Tsushima Strait.

As invaders have often discovered, Korea becomes more mountainous the further north you go. The mountains are not very high, rising to about 2750m (9000ft), but the central spinal Taebaek range is composed of those characteristically steep-sided hills that dominated so much of the fighting during 1950–53. In the south of Korea, the mountains lose their harshness. The river valleys of the Han, the Kum, and the Naktong are old centres of Korean civilisation. These rivers provided successive defence lines for the embattled United Nations forces during the fluid fighting of 1950–51.

Given these geographical factors, the Korean people, who are a distinct racial stock, have always been aware that their country stands at a critical strategic crossroads of the Far East. In particular, Korea has always been a land bridge between China and Japan, between the dominant continental and the dominant maritime powers of northeast Asia. Traditionally, Korea has always been envisaged by the Japanese as 'a dagger pointed at the heart of Japan', while the Chinese have defined the peninsula as 'a hammer ready to strike at the head of China'.

With the establishment of a virtual US protectorate over Japan in 1945, and the military partition of Korea between the US and the Soviet Union at the same time, all four major powers in the Far East had become involved in Korea. So the strategic perception of Korea as a country at the crossroads of the Far East became even more complex.

Since 1945 these great-power rivalries in the region have become increasingly intensified by the speed-up in global communications, by the existence of nuclear weapons, and by the persisting tension between the US and the Soviet Union. Peking, Tokyo, and Vladivostok all lie within 1600km (1000 miles) of Seoul, the South Korean capital. Moreover, with the single exception of western and central Europe, there is probably today a greater concentration of military forces in and around Korea than in any other contested area in the world. These tensions, historical and contemporary, precipitated the Korean War.

For many centuries under both the Koryo dynasty (936–1392) and the Yi dynasty (1392–1910) Korea was a united kingdom holding tributary status within the Confucian system of the Chinese Empire. Like China, Korea suffered the Mongol invasions of the 13th century. But Korean civilisation continued to flourish until the devastating invasion by the Japanese leader Toyotomi Hideyoshi in 1592.

His intention was to march into China through Korea. But Chinese armies crossed the Yalu River (as in 1950) to intervene in Korea. After six years Hideyoshi was repulsed but he took back to Japan many scholars and artisans and Korean culture never again achieved its predominance in the region.

Isolation and annexation

In 1636, the Ching (or Manchu) rulers of China invaded Korea and forced the country to acknowledge the supremacy of this new Chinese dynasty. But the demands of the Ching were not onerous, and only a token tribute was sent annually from Korea via Mukden to Peking. However, the Korean kingdom decided to cut itself off from external contacts apart from China, and thus the so-called 'hermit kingdom' came into being.

The tributary ritual which symbolised Korea's political status lasted until the 1860s. But her self-imposed isolation (and resistance to modernisation) weakened when faced with a resurgent Japan after the Meiji restoration of 1868. There was also a threat from the north, for in 1860 the Russian Empire seized the Manchu lands north and east of the Amur River, so giving the Russians a short, 18km (11-mile) border with northeastern Korea.

A historic triangular conflict now developed between China, Japan, and Russia for the control of Korea. Simultaneously, Western influence began to percolate into the country, especially after treaty relations were developed with the United States, Great Britain and other Western powers after 1882. These foreign influences further weakened the traditional Confucian ethical system which was still dominant in Korea.

The showdown between China and Japan over Korea came during 1894–5. Japanese troops landed at Inchon, on the Korean west coast, and swept northwards through Pyongyang to the Yalu area. The Japanese navy destroyed the Chinese fleet and China was thus eliminated from the contest to dominate Korea. By the Treaty of Shimonoseki (17 April 1895) the Chinese Empire recognised Korean independence.

An even more intense and significant struggle now developed between Japan and Russia for the control of Korea and with it supremacy in northeast Asia. The Russians hoped to establish a warm-water port at Masan, in southeast Korea (where US Marines stopped the North Korean advance in August 1950). The Russians were also active in Manchuria, and extended their influence from there into northern Korea. Japan viewed all these developments with great alarm.

The tensions exploded into war in 1904.

Once again the Japanese landed at Inchon. They then advanced across the Yalu River into Manchuria and eventually captured Port Arthur, the Russian base. The Tsarist armies in the region were defeated at Mukden, while Admiral Togo annihilated the Russian fleet in the Tsushima Strait between Japan and Korea. In the Treaty of Portsmouth, New Hampshire (5 September 1905), Russia acknowledged Japan's 'paramount political, military, and economic interests' in Korea. Both the United States and Great Britain specifically granted Japan a free hand in Korea at this time. The country became a Japanese protectorate.

In 1910 Japan formally abolished the ancient Yi dynasty, pensioned off the last Korean king, and formally annexed Korea, which now became the 'Chosen Government-General', a Japanese colony.

Above: Japan decisively asserted herself over China in the Far East during the Sino-Japanese War of 1894–5. In this war, the Japanese ended Chinese influence in the Korean peninsula. The decisive battle, illustrated in the painting here, was a naval action in the Yellow Sea, which saw the Japanese fleet win a convincing victory.
Above left: The Japanese attack on Port Arthur, on the night of 8/9 February 1904, the beginning of the next great expansionist war fought by the Japanese; this time their foe was the Russian Empire, with its enormous resources and modern fleet. Once again, however, the Japanese triumphed and destroyed Russian naval pretensions at the battle of Tsushima in 1905. This success led to direct Japanese control of Korea.

Japanese rule was harsh, but Tokyo claimed that it brought modernisation and efficiency. The infrastructure of a modern state was indeed created under Japanese rule, and there began a process of partial industrialisation, especially in northern Korea.

But Koreans continued to resent Japanese rule. The anti-Japanese demonstrations of 1 March 1919 were crushed by the government. But in their wake a Korean Provisional Government-in-Exile was established in China. A Korean Communist Party was formed in Seoul during 1925, but was soon forced underground by the Japanese security police. Other Korean communists found a role helping the Chinese communists in the 1930s, while some fought the Japanese as partisans using Manchurian and Soviet territory as sanctuary. One of these partisans was Kim Il Sung, who later became the Soviet-backed ruler of North Korea.

What all Korean dissidents had in common was the hope that Japan's defeat in the Pacific War would lead to Korean independence. But what was not appreciated was that the involved circumstances of Japan's defeat would immediately lead to the partition of the country for the first time in its history.

Korea divided

The question of Korea's postwar status was discussed at the Cairo conference of November 1943. Subsequently the Cairo Declaration by Roosevelt, Churchill and Chiang Kai-shek stated that 'mindful of the enslavement of Korea' they were determined that 'in due course Korea shall become free and independent'. Roosevelt favoured a trusteeship arrangement for the country and there was a tentative agreement to this effect between him and Stalin at the Yalta conference in February 1945. China and perhaps Britain were also envisaged as trustees.

Events soon precluded any trusteeship arrangement. Following Roosevelt's death in April 1945, President Harry Truman was increasingly uneasy over Soviet intentions in the Far East. News of the successful testing of the atomic bomb reached Truman at the Potsdam conference in July 1945, and his primary motive in deciding to use the weapon against Japan was to save American lives. But he also hoped that the bomb might end the Pacific War so quickly that a Soviet invasion of Manchuria and Korea might not be necessary.

All such hopes vanished with the speed of the Russian reaction to the atomic attack on Hiroshima (6 August 1945). The Soviets declared war against Japan on 8 August; they also accepted the Cairo and Potsdam Declarations which committed them to Korean independence. But on 9 August Soviet military operations on an enormous scale were under way in the Far East. Manchuria was invaded by three Russian army groups, there were landings on South Sakhalin, and an invasion force for the Kuriles was prepared. On 10 August, Soviet troops landed at Unggi in northeast Korea. There were further Soviet landings within the next few days at Chongjin and Nanam, and by 16 August the Russians were in Wonsan, the biggest port on the Korean eastern seaboard.

Japan had made its first surrender offer on 10 August. Immediately the US War Department in the Pentagon began drafting surrender procedures. 'General Order No 1' would be issued to Tokyo to define the capitulation zones in all theatres of the Pacific War. That same day, Secretary of State James Byrnes instructed the State-War-Navy Coordinating Committee to prepare a plan for a joint Soviet-American occupation of Korea 'with the line as far north as possible'.

During the night of 10/11 August the task of drafting the surrender arrangements for Korea devolved on Colonel Charles H. Bonesteel, the Chief of the Policy Section of the Strategy and Policy Group of the US Army Operations Division. With him was Colonel Dean Rusk (then on active service in the Operations Division). Time was of the essence, and as the only map available in his Pentagon office was a small-scale wall map of the Far East, Bonesteel decided to use the 38th parallel as north–south demarcation. Seoul and Inchon were thus placed in the US zone; it was envisaged that a centralised administration of Korea would eventually emerge.

The 38th parallel thus became part of the final draft of General Order No 1 which was then cleared by the Joint Chiefs of Staff (JCS) and by President Truman

on 15 August 1945, VJ-Day. The order was also cleared by the British, Soviet, and Chinese governments and cabled to General Douglas MacArthur in Manila; as Allied Supreme Commander he would issue the surrender order to the defeated Japanese imperial government. These hurried arrangements were of great significance as they legitimised the military partition of Korea.

Meanwhile, Soviet troops had entered Pyongyang on 24 August and quickly

pushed on towards the 38th parallel. On 2 September MacArthur took the Japanese surrender in Tokyo Bay. But it was not until 8 September that US forces from Okinawa landed at Inchon. The next day, in a formal ceremony in Seoul, General John R. Hodge accepted the surrender of all Japanese forces south of the 38th parallel. So ended the Japanese era in Korea; but the country was already divided between the two leading powers of the postwar world.

The two Koreas

The 38th parallel was of course an artificial line which sliced through ancient Korean provinces, dividing the mainly agricultural south of the country from the partly industrialised north. There were about 9 million people in the Russian zone, and about 21 million in the US zone. The Soviet military quickly sealed off their zone and stopped all trade and traffic with the southern zone. By the end of 1945 there was a *de facto* frontier dividing Korea.

The wartime allies now made an attempt to unify Korea. At the Moscow Foreign Ministers' Conference in December 1945 the United States, Britain and the Soviet Union agreed on the formation of a provisional Korean government. But the agreement also stipulated that there should be a five-year trusteeship under the three powers at the conference, plus China. A Joint Commission composed of

the two commands in Korea was to assist in the setting-up of the Korean government through consultation with the Korean political parties.

There was widespread Korean nationalist opposition to the trusteeship proposals. When the Joint Commission met in Seoul in March 1946, the Soviet side insisted that only those Koreans who agreed with the trusteeship proposals could consult with the Commission. This was unacceptable to the American side on broad democratic grounds and the Joint Commission adjourned in May 1946.

The adjournment of the Joint Commission hastened moves towards the creation of two separate Korean governments. On the wider stage of world politics, East and West were increasingly polarised after a series of disagreements over Iran, Greece, Germany and many other issues. Early in 1947 the United States once again tried to seek a Korean agreement through the Joint Commission, which convened for the second time in Seoul in May. But the talks were again stalemated over the Soviet refusal to consult with the opponents of the trusteeship proposals. By July 1947, the two sides had found it impossible to agree on a joint report, and it was clear that further negotiations were futile.

By now the wartime alliance had yielded to the Cold War and events in Korea increasingly reflected the fundamental differences that seemed to divide the Western governments and the Soviet Union. With no prospect of Korean

independence or unification, the US government turned the entire issue over to the United Nations in September 1947. The UN was now increasingly concerned with events in Korea.

An embryonic North Korean state was already in existence. The Soviets had chosen as their local leader the former guerrilla fighter, Kim Il Sung, who had been active along the Korean-Manchurian border in the 1930s. Although his precise links with the Soviet government during the Second World War are a matter of conjecture, he was reported to have landed at Wonsan in September 1945 in the uniform of a Soviet major. During the following month, October 1945, Kim was elected the First Secretary of the 'North Korean Central Bureau of the Korean Communist Party'.

With Soviet support Kim Il Sung soon eliminated his opponents both within and outside the Communist Party in North Korea. During February 1946 he became chairman of the 'Provisional People's Committee' of North Korea. This was a Soviet-backed government which organised a system of controls analogous to those imposed on the Eastern European countries under Soviet occupation at that time.

In August 1946, Kim Il Sung further consolidated his power when he presided over the amalgamation of the Communist Party and the New People's Party, which was a pro-Chinese communist group composed of Koreans who had spent the

The speed of the Soviet advance in the Far East during their August 1945 offensive (above and below) meant that they were established   Korea by the time of the Japanese surrender. Below right : General MacArthur signs the formal surrender document on board the USS Missouri on 2 September 1945.

war at Mao Tse-tung's base at Yenan. In the new North Korean Workers' Party – as the Communist Party was now known – Kim was vice-chairman. But he remained the indispensable link between the party and the Soviet military. Thus the 'amalgamation' of the two parties was really a takeover of the less reliable Yenan elements.

In South Korea, the road to separate statehood was rather more complicated, as befitted a pluralistic society. But after a process of trial and error, the US military government created in October 1946 the South Korean Interim Legislative Assembly. Half of the assembly were elected, half appointed. The assembly was dominated by the followers of the veteran Korean nationalist, Syngman Rhee.

Although Rhee faced considerable opposition within South Korea, he was helped both by the reference of the Korean problem to the United Nations and by his willingness to work with the Americans on the basis of a separate South Korean government. On 14 November 1947, the UN General Assembly adopted

a resolution which provided a programme for Korean independence and unification.

The resolution called for free, all-Korea elections, and the creation of a UN Temporary Commission on Korea to supervise these elections. The UN also called for the creation of a Korean national government after the elections, which would then form its own security forces to replace the two military commands in Korea.

As the Soviet military refused to allow the UN Temporary Commission to enter North Korea, free elections took place in South Korea alone during May 1948. Following these elections, an assembly was convened, a constitution drafted, and on 20 July 1948 Syngman Rhee was elected president of the Republic of Korea (ROK). The new government formally took over on 15 August 1948 with the termination of US military government. But US troops remained in South Korea until June 1949, when the last contingents sailed from Inchon.

In December 1948, four months after the creation of the Republic of Korea, the UN General Assembly declared that 'a lawful government' had been established in South Korea. Following this imprimatur, the United States and other countries recognised the ROK in the early months of 1949. These developments were of great importance, for they gave the United Nations a direct stake in the continued existence of the ROK.

Meanwhile, in Pyongyang the 'Democratic People's Republic of Korea' had been proclaimed on 9 September 1948, with Kim Il Sung as its prime minister. A few weeks later the Soviet Union declared that its troops would be withdrawn from North Korea, although a strong force of Soviet advisers remained.

Kim Il Sung's position as Korea's communist leader was finally formalised in June 1949 when the North and the South Korean Workers' Parties were merged to form a single Korean Workers' Party under Kim's chairmanship. Kim thus became the leader of the all-Korean party and of the North Korean government.

Now two opposed Korean regimes, representing hostile interests and beliefs, and both claiming jurisdiction over all Korea, faced each other along the 38th parallel.

The North Korean build-up

From the very beginnings of the two Korean states there was not only tension along the 38th parallel but throughout most of the peninsula. President Rhee called rhetorically for a march north (*Puk Chin*), but Pyongyang was able to back its own reunification strategy with considerable military pressure. In late 1948 a series of communist-led revolts in the southern provinces of the ROK quickly developed into a guerrilla campaign with the object of toppling the Seoul regime.

The insurgency was counterproductive. The atrocities committed by the insurgents alienated public opinion, land reform removed popular discontent, and the ROK army and constabulary developed effective counter-insurgency techniques. By the end of 1949, even a Soviet

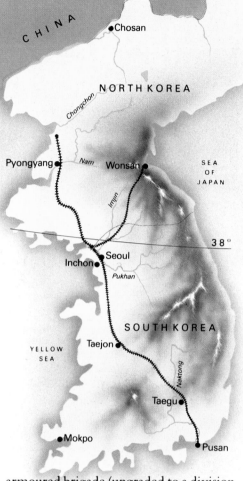

source noted that the communist threat in South Korea had 'markedly subsided'.

Another factor in the defeat of the communist insurgency was the pace of the economic recovery in South Korea. Under the sponsorship of the US Economic Cooperation Administration, significant gains were reported during 1948–50 in coal mining, textiles, railway construction and fisheries. South Korea was self-supporting agriculturally, and industrial production generally increased.

The Soviet viewpoint

The winter of 1949–50 was a critical period in view of later events. It was now that Pyongyang's reunification strategy moved from guerrilla warfare to the planning of an outright conventional invasion of the South. Following Premier Kim Il Sung's visit to Moscow in March 1949, when he conferred with Stalin, the Soviet press had already stressed that North Korea could expect 'all-round' assistance from the Soviet Union.

During the early months of 1950, North Korea received large shipments of modern military equipment from Russia, including about 150 T34 tanks, over 100 Yak fighter aircraft and other heavy military equipment, including artillery. The North Koreans had begun recruiting for this army as early as 1946–7, and all units had received Soviet training and Soviet arms before the accelerated build-up of early 1950.

By this time, the Korean People's Army (KPA) was a well-trained force which could field about 135,000 men organised into seven infantry divisions and an armoured brigade (upgraded to a division in July 1950). There was also a heavily indoctrinated border constabulary together with independent assault units. Each infantry division had an organic artillery regiment of 122mm howitzers, as well as a battalion of self-propelled 76mm guns.

In an Asian context, this was a highly effective, Soviet-model army. The ROK army, on the other hand, was little more than an upgraded paramilitary force. It numbered about 95,000 men in June 1950, armed with mortars and light artillery, but it possessed no tanks. Of its eight divisions, only four were deployed near the 38th parallel.

As the KPA moved to the parallel in early 1950, Pyongyang stepped up its political warfare. In his 1950 New Year Address, Kim Il Sung called on South Koreans to destroy the Rhee regime

'from within and without . . . and incessantly support the guerrillas both morally and materially'. These exhortations had the effect of concentrating both South Korean and US attention on the fading guerrilla threat in the South rather than on the mounting preparations in North Korea for a conventional invasion.

This emphasis on the guerrilla threat was a distraction from the rising tempo of border incidents along the 38th parallel during 1949–50. Initially, border raids had been carried out by both armies. But in both May and July 1949 North Korean units crossed the parallel in some force near Kaesong. The South Korean town of Ongjin, in the far west of the Republic, but detached from the rest of the country by the Yellow Sea, was another focus of border fighting.

During this skirmishing, which was conducted up to battalion level, the North Koreans were always pushed back north of the parallel. But by early 1950 there was a rising intensity to these border raids as artillery duels became commonplace right along the parallel from the Yellow Sea to the Sea of Japan. Another centre of border fighting was the large town of Chunchon, on the central ROK front.

By the spring of 1950, border incidents had become so prevalent that no special significance was ascribed to them in Seoul by either the South Korean government or the United States. By their frequency these incidents thus provided an excellent cover for the very real preparations in the North for the invasion planned for 25 June 1950.

On 3 June 1950, as North Korean units filtered into the hills north of the 38th

Far left: The Korean peninsula, showing the strategic importance of Korea (lying between the three powers of Japan, China and the Soviet Union) and the 38th parallel of latitude along which the country was divided in 1945. Centre left: South Korean local defence forces. Poorly armed and with little military training, such units were hardly a threat to the well armed North Korean Army. Left: Mao Tse-tung reads the proclamation of the Chinese People's Republic in October 1949. The triumph of the communists in China was to be crucial to the outbreak of the Korean War.

parallel, the Pyongyang 'Democratic Front for the Attainment of the Unification of the Fatherland' launched a new, intensive campaign for the 'peaceful unification' of Korea through free elections. Representatives from the North were sent into the South to bolster the campaign. On 19 June, the 'Supreme People's Assembly' in Pyongyang repeated the call for 'peaceful unification' through elections.

There can be little doubt that moves by the 'Democratic Front' were part of a carefully planned deception campaign which helped to lull the South Koreans into a false sense of security on the very eve of the invasion. When these 'peaceful unification' measures were proposed, the North Korean invasion plans were complete. Documents later captured by UN forces in Korea included the attack orders for the KPA's 4th Division, which was scheduled to push down the Uijongbu corridor to Seoul. These orders, drafted in Russian for the Divisional Chief of Staff, had been issued on 22 June 1950. When the invasion came on 25 June, it achieved complete tactical and strategic surprise.

There are complex reasons for the complete surprise achieved by the North Korean invasion. The secrecy of the North Korean build-up and the effectiveness of the deception campaign were only partly responsible. In fact, many of the details of the communist build-up had been reported to MacArthur's Far Eastern Command in Tokyo. This command

kept a secret Intelligence Unit, the 'Korean Liaison Office', in Seoul.

Perhaps the most important reason for the intelligence failure was the downgrading of Korea in American defence priorities. Ever since late 1947, the US Joint Chiefs of Staff (JCS) had ruled that any significant military commitment to South Korea was impractical in view of American global responsibilities. In the later Stalin period it was understandable why the primary threat seemed to be in Europe, in the Middle East, or perhaps against Tito's Yugoslavia. This overall view had been stated in Secretary of State Dean Acheson's famous speech of 12 January 1950 in which he outlined the US 'defense perimeter' in the Pacific. Japan was included within the perimeter, but not South Korea.

Despite many reports during 1949–50 of the gradual massing of North Korean forces, imminent invasion was not considered probable. These agent reports included details of KPA troop movements, the evacuation of civilians immediately north of the 38th parallel, concentration of armoured units, and removal of civilian traffic from the Wonsan–Chorwon railway. This was a key logistic route supplying the central sector above the parallel.

One of the official US Army historians of the Korean War, Colonel James F. Schnabel, was assigned to MacArthur's HQ in Tokyo during the years 1949–50. He has written that: '. . . by late 1949, talk of a North Korean invasion was almost routine in intelligence circles. By early

1950, there was a pattern of growing urgency. But it went undetected, or at least unheeded, against the more riotous background of threatening Communist behaviour in other parts of the world – in Asia, in Western Europe, and the Middle East.'

It was Secretary of State Acheson who summed up this historic intelligence failure during the prolonged congressional hearings following General MacArthur's relief in April 1951. Acheson testified that the State Department, the Army Department, the CIA and the Far East Command '. . . were in agreement that the possibility for an attack on the Korean Republic existed at this time, but they were all in agreement that its launching in the summer of 1950 did not appear imminent'. Instead, a revival of North Korea's insurgency against the South was expected. It was at this high level that North Korean intentions were miscalculated and her capabilities ignored.

At 0400 hours on 25 June 1950 the North Korean offensive was launched south across the parallel. After a massive artillery barrage against key points, communist tanks and infantry struck south along the main routes to Seoul and other South Korean cities. It very soon became clear that this was no border raid. Accordingly, at about 0900 hours the US ambassador in Seoul, John J. Muccio, signalled the State Department that an 'all-out offensive against the Republic of Korea' had begun. The preliminaries to the Korean War were over.

1. The Attack from the North

It was the abruptness and unexpected power of the attack by the North Korean Army (KPA) that gave it such an initial advantage in the days following its assault across the 38th Parallel on 25 June 1950.

Preceded by a long and intensive barrage of artillery and mortar fire the tanks of the KPA's armoured division lunged forward with frightening speed, smashing headlong into totally unprepared and gravely ill-equipped units of the army of the Republic of Korea (ROK). The weight of the communist attack was concentrated to the west of the great Taebaek mountain range whose spine runs the full length of the Korean peninsula. Its main thrust was against the South Korean capital city of Seoul which lay, invitingly, only a few kilometres south of the 38th parallel.

As the KPA crossed the frontier it quickly became obvious that its forces were geared to develop no less than four spearheads pressing forward on very narrow fronts. These spearheads were quite prepared to bypass resistance if necessary in order to make rapid headway southwards. The KPA was determined to capitalise to the full on the total initial surprise which had been achieved.

In the west a lightning strike into the Ongin peninsula by the KPA 6th Division soon overwhelmed the town. Because of its isolated position it was scarcely possible to reinforce it. Further to the east one thrust by the KPA 1st Division was discerned making for the town of Kaesong while eastwards again the KPA 3rd and 4th Divisions together with the 105th Tank Division raced full tilt down the Uijongbu corridor towards Seoul itself.

This was an easy route which lay through low hills and followed the grain of the country. Historically it was the most frequently chosen route of armies from the north seeking to take Seoul.

Amphibious assaults

East of the mountains of the Taebaek range (which at the 38th parallel almost hug Korea's eastern shore) another assault was in progress. Following the narrow coastal strip and utilising amphibious landings to hasten their progress, the 5th Division of the KPA made for the South Korean coastal towns of Kangnung and Samchok.

During the first four days of the war the KPA advanced nonstop without

Opposite page: Communist propaganda showing their soldiers as all-conquering heroes, capturing dispirited US prisoners, and surging on to victory. In fact, the communist troops who undertook the invasion of the South were in general better equipped than their South Korean counterparts in the ROK, and their equipment was very much as shown here – Soviet-built for the most part, like the T34 tanks, and the PPSh sub-machine guns carried by the soldiers on the tanks. Above: Soldiers of the ROK being inspected in 1949, during a visit of the US Military Advisory Group of Korea.

meeting any real opposition. Here and there an isolated ROK army position would put up some resistance, but the arrival of the North Korean tanks would always put them to flight. The totally disproportionate odds in both manpower and equipment meant that the ROK army could not even hope to delay the enemy. They had neither tanks nor anti-tank weapons capable of stopping the Russian-built T34 tanks with their highly effective 85mm guns.

The North Koreans used their tanks to maximum effect against such an ill-equipped army and this helped to maintain the momentum of the KPA advance. Using any available road or track the tanks would spearhead the advance by driving fast in line-ahead formation. If they encountered enemy resistance they would press straight onto and through the ROK army positions almost as if they did not exist. Following on behind the tanks the infantry would move to both flanks of the enemy positions, closing in together in the rear to trap those that remained behind.

Given that they had absolutely nothing which they could use to knock out the KPA tanks as they rumbled into their positions the ROK army units frequently disintegrated as men fled to save their lives. It is scarcely surprising that in the first week of the war no fewer than 34,000 men of the ROK army were reported as missing.

The South Korean capital was captured on 28 June and the government was transferred only just in time to the town of Taejon to the south and in the centre of the country. Having occupied Seoul the North Koreans halted their advance briefly in order to regroup and to allow their administrative 'tail' to catch up. In retrospect it might be said that this halt on the part of the KPA, although necessary, was ultimately to lead to its undoing. The short breathing-space allowed to the South gave time for the shattered ROK divisions to be concentrated and re-formed. More important still, it gave the

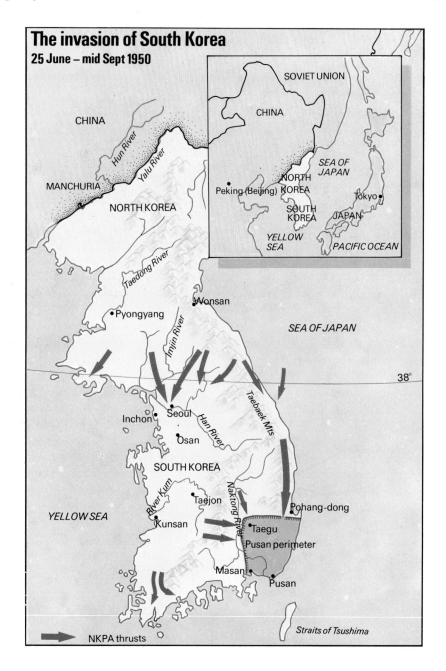

The invasion of South Korea
25 June – mid Sept 1950

CHINA

SOVIET UNION

CHINA

Hun River

Yalu River

MANCHURIA

NORTH KOREA

SEA OF JAPAN

Peking (Beijing)

NORTH KOREA

SOUTH KOREA

Tokyo

JAPAN

YELLOW SEA

PACIFIC OCEAN

Taedong River

Wonsan

Pyongyang

Imjin River

SEA OF JAPAN

38°

Taebaek Mts

Inchon

Seoul

Han River

Osan

SOUTH KOREA

River Kum

Naktong River

Taejon

Pohang-dong

YELLOW SEA

Kunsan

Taegu

Pusan perimeter

Masan

Pusan

NKPA thrusts

Straits of Tsushima

Western world a chance to respond – and they intervened only in the nick of time.

The Secretary-General of the United Nations, Trygve Lie, was told of the North Korean invasion at 3am (New York time) on 25 June. He instantly summoned a UN Security Council meeting which assembled at 2pm the same day. By a unanimous vote (the Soviet Union was not present – see page 68) the Security Council condemned the North Koreans for committing an unprovoked act of aggression and, further, called on the KPA to cease fire and withdraw northwards across the 38th parallel.

There was no response and the Security Council met again on 27 June and called upon all member nations of the UN to bring support to the Republic of Korea. This rapid and positive reaction from the

world organisation provided a lead which the Western nations were quick to follow. They recognised only too well the disastrous consequences which would result if the whole of the strategically vital Korean peninsula were to fall into North Korean, and thus effectively Soviet hands.

The United States reacted with great speed. Immediately following the UN call for assistance President Truman announced that military aid would straightaway be given to South Korea. He gave orders for the US Navy to go into action in Korean waters and for the US Air Force to fly missions north of the 38th parallel from their bases in Japan.

Two days later, on 29 June, the US president made the critically important decision to involve US ground forces in Korea. He granted authority to General Douglas MacArthur to send units to Korea from the US forces employed on occupation duties in Japan. With forces committed to the land battle in Korea there was no going back for the USA.

On the same day General MacArthur flew to Korea in order to see for himself what the situation was and how, if his forces were to become involved, they could best be used. He ignored extremely bad weather reports for the flight route and the fact that the airfield of Suwon where he intended to land was under attack from North Korean aircraft even as he took off from Japan. It was typical of the man.

When the war in Korea broke out MacArthur held three major appointments:

Supreme Commander Allied Powers in Japan; Commander-in-Chief, Far East, over all US forces in the west Pacific; and Commanding General, US Army in the Far East. His immense authority, born of his World War II exploits in the Pacific, was to become a major factor in the developments of this new major international conflict.

His fleeting visit to the front line confirmed him in his belief that if the North Koreans were to be prevented from occupying the whole of Korea then American forces would have to intervene – rapidly and on a major scale. In his report to the Pentagon, which arrived in Washington on 30 June, MacArthur requested permission to dispatch two divisions to Korea from the US occupation forces in Japan. Approval came from the president the same day.

At that time there were four US divisions on occupation duties in Japan. To-

Opposite page left: The routes taken by the KPA during its invasion of the South in 1950. Opposite page right: An ROK infantryman moves up to the front.
Top: The population moved south as the communist forces pushed their way down the peninsula, gathering belongings and fleeing before the victorious North Korean army.
Above: The UN Commission on Korea meets in 1951. It was the prompt offer of UN assistance, and the swift intervention of US forces under the UN flag that saved South Korea from conquest by the North.

Top: A Korean family rebuild their home after the ravages of the war have passed. Above: Relatives identify the bodies of 300 South Koreans killed during the Northern advance. Opposite page top: US artillery fires in support of ROK ground forces. At this stage of the war, however, US support was not sufficient to stem the tide of communist victories. Opposite page centre: General Douglas MacArthur, that doughty warrior who set out to hold the South with all his considerable expertise and energy. Opposite page bottom: A Vought F4U Corsair about to take off. As US involvement grew in scope, it included the use of the Seventh Fleet to attack targets on the Korean mainland.

gether they formed the US Eighth Army. Without exception these divisions were understrength, poorly trained, physically unfit and extremely badly armed and equipped. The best of the four was the US 24th Infantry Division and it was the first to go to Korea. The remaining divisions were trawled to find men to enhance the strength of the 24th, and in the same way each successive division had its numbers bolstered up by drafts from those remaining.

The first fighting unit of the US Army to arrive in Korea from Japan was a task force made up of two companies of the 1st Battalion, 21st Infantry Regiment of 24th Infantry Division. Task Force Smith, as it was known, took its name from the commanding officer of the battalion, Lieutenant-Colonel Charles B. Smith. He was warned of the impending move to Korea on the evening of 30 June. By 1100 hours the next day the task force had arrived in Korea where they boarded trains to take them northwards to Taejon. Their final destination was to the north of a small town called Osan, where their orders were to establish a defensive position astride the main road south from Seoul. There their task was to delay the North Korean advance as long as possible to allow further US troops to be deployed.

Task Force Smith was only just in time. They arrived at their positions at 0300 hours on 5 July and as dawn broke they saw coming towards them along the road from the north a long column of tanks followed in the distance by lorried and then marching infantry.

The KPA had had problems after the capture of Seoul. They had to cross the River Han to continue their thrust southwards but they needed first to establish a bridgehead with infantry before their tanks could cross. However, the ROK army was able to deal with KPA infantry when the latter were not supported by tanks so the river crossing was a slow and bloody business.

Now their next opponents were to be the US Task Force Smith. As they approached Osan some 30km (19 miles) south of the River Han, they encountered Smith's positions. Following normal practice the column of tanks drove on along the road in line-ahead straight through and beyond the US troops. Nothing that the Americans had would stop them. The 2.36-in bazookas of the infantry were quite incapable of penetrating the armour of the T34/85 tanks, and Smith's artillery support, firing directly at the tanks, saw their high-explosive shells bounce off the hulls without effect. Only high explosive anti-tank (HEAT) shells did any damage and Task Force Smith had only been issued with six of these rounds!

A fighting retreat

Notwithstanding these difficulties, Smith's men delayed the enemy infantry for up to five hours and only then was the order to withdraw given to avoid being overrun by the enemy. The Americans left carrying only their rifles, abandoning all heavy weapons and vehicles where they stood.

Behind Colonel Smith's positions the remainder of 24th Division were now deployed. They succeeded in delaying the North Koreans so that it took them a week to cover the 65km (40 miles) to the next major obstacle which faced them: the Kum River. Here the Americans sought to establish a defensive line to protect the city of Taejon to the south.

Meanwhile the major US effort to support South Korea was rapidly getting under way. On 10 July General MacArthur was appointed Commander-in-Chief United Nations Command (CINCUNC) and on 13 July Lieutenant-General Walton H. Walker (one of Patton's corps commanders in Europe in

divisions deployed to the east of the 24th to fight tenaciously against the other main KPA thrusts via Chunju and along the east coast towards Pohang-dong. Delays were forced on the enemy and many valiant actions were fought but the KPA nonetheless remorselessly pressed on southwards.

The vanguard of two KPA divisions arrived on the Kum River on 13 July. The river line was thinly defended by two regiments of the 24th Division. The river posed less of an obstacle than the Americans had hoped, as in many places it had dried out. The North Korean tanks and infantry crossed it with ease, and the latter, moving round the Americans' flanks, were soon poised to envelop the US positions. General Dean ordered his regiments to withdraw and they made their way back into Taejon itself. There Dean intended to make a stand.

The KPA formed up and began its assault on the city on 19 July. Tanks again led the attack but this time carrying infantry with them. Already tired and dispirited by their unsuccessful actions to the north, the 24th Division prepared to fight it out. General Dean worked avidly to build up the morale of his men. He moved from command post to command post instilling confidence by his very

World War II) established his Eighth US Army in Korea (EUSAK). From that time onwards Walker commanded all UN forces in Korea.

Walker's chief aim was to use the 24th Division to slow down the main KPA advance down the Seoul–Taejon axis. If he could succeed in doing this there would be time for two further divisions from Japan, the 25th Infantry Division and the 1st Cavalry Division (acting in the infantry role), to arrive and deploy. Not only was it essential for the 24th Division under Major-General William F. Dean to hold the enemy at the Kum River, but Walker was also relying on the ROK

presence. Just at this moment the division was at last issued with a new anti-tank weapon: 3.5in rocket-launchers were flown in from Japan. These had been developed towards the end of World War II but only now had the ammunition been perfected.

Tank hunting

Dean saw immediately that this weapon could be effective against the hitherto all-powerful enemy tanks. He personally organised groups of his men into tank-hunting parties and they proved to be extremely successful. During the course of the battle for Taejon they knocked out at least 15 tanks and Dean personally led one hunter group which stalked a tank for over an hour through the crumbling city until it was eventually immobilised.

But the inevitable happened: exhausted and dejected, the 24th Division was finally driven from Taejon. With the town virtually surrounded, many men were taken prisoner as they withdrew. Dean himself, though he remained free for a month, roaming in the hills near the city, was eventually captured, and thus earned the unenviable distinction of being the senior US officer to be taken by the North Koreans during the war.

Taejon fell to the enemy on 20 July but the desperate delaying tactics of the 24th Division had not been in vain. The 25th Division had landed in Korea between 10 and 15 July and the 1st Cavalry Division came ashore at Pohang-dong on the east coast on 18 July. By 22 July both divisions were deployed in battle positions: in itself a remarkable logistical achievement.

The 25th Division was given the task of supporting the hard-pressed ROK troops in the centre of the country in the area of Sangju almost due east of Taejon. The enemy attack developed against the division on 26 July and was sustained through to the end of the month. The newly arrived division was then forced to initiate its first withdrawal.

The 1st Cavalry Division took over from the battered 24th Division south of Taejon. It moved into positions in and around Yongdong as the last elements of General Dean's division passed through. Still in close pursuit, the KPA arrived in

front of Yongdong on 23 July and the 1st Cavalry Division received its first bitter taste of the North Korean medicine. Using their usual tactics of skirting round the flanks of the American positions the KPA forced the first withdrawal of US units by 25 July, but the area generally was held until Major-General Gay, commanding general of the 1st Cavalry Division, issued orders on 29 July to vacate the town to take up new positions in the area of Kumchong.

The events of the last few days of July caused General Walker grave anxiety. Communications within his command were at best intermittent and he never possessed up-to-date information con-

Top: The mountainous terrain of much of the Korean peninsula was of little hindrance to the KPA, which soon became expert at using high ground to outflank its foes.
Above: US troops pass a knocked-out T34/85 tank. The US forces found that they could inflict heavy losses on the KPA, but during this early stage of the war the KPA was always able to swing round the flanks of US formations, and force them to pull back.
Opposite page: Fifty-one victims of North Korean atrocities are uncovered in a mass grave. They had been killed near Chonju soon after the first wave of KPA advances.

cerning the situation along the whole length of his front. What fragmentary reports he did receive gave him little comfort. The stark reality was that the arrival of US troops had done little to slow down the impetus of the North Korean drive. An experienced soldier, he knew that he could do little to remedy the deficiencies of his men's equipment. Where he thought he could do something was in the area that worried him most. He felt sure that his troops were too easily giving up territory to the enemy: not putting up enough of a fight. While recognising the poor quality of equipment, the lack of training and the shortage of good leaders at all levels that posed difficulties for his commanders, he nonetheless made a tour of all divisional command posts and in a characteristically aggressive manner put his thoughts across to his generals. Units were to stabilise the front line and be prepared to initiate offensive action whenever possible. Should tactical withdrawals be necessary contact with the enemy must be maintained: this latter point was in reference to the all-too-frequent hasty withdrawals made at all levels by units seeking, before they had even made contact with the enemy, to extricate them-

selves from possible encirclement by enemy infantry. The substance of his orders was soon encapsulated in the expression 'stand or die'. The tactic of trading space for time was leading to the inevitable: space was running out and any further extensive withdrawal would find the UN forces literally with their backs to the sea.

Blunting the rapier

General Walker now had the 25th Division and the 1st Cavalry Division in position, attempting to blunt the edge of the KPA's rapier thrust down the main axis from Seoul through to Pusan. To the right of these divisions ROK troops were confronted by less powerful thrusts and yet were being forced slowly but constantly southwards. Now a further and extremely serious threat revealed itself. As the North Koreans seized Taejon a complete division of the KPA was withdrawn from the main battle and diverted to swing out widely to the west to outflank the American positions, then to turn eastwards and strike for Pusan itself. The division made rapid progress and met virtually no opposition. By 24 July it had

concentrated in the area of Sunchon, preparatory to advancing along the south coast. It was at this moment that the seriousness of the situation was realised by General Walker, and he ordered his only reserve, the battered 24th Division, southwards in a desperate effort to block the move. Elements of the 25th Division were also sent south as they were freed by the contraction of the front further north.

This right-hook manoeuvre continued to the end of July unhindered, and leading elements of the KPA division were by that time within the area of Masan, only 50km (30 miles) from Pusan. Then in the first two days of August regiments of the 25th Division arrived and successfully deployed in positions from which they brought the enemy's headlong drive to a halt.

The ease with which this North Korean division swept round the American flank well illustrates a major problem for the UN forces. The KPA's tactic of outflanking formations holding good defensive positions was really only successful because the UN forces were so thin on the ground. That the UN positions could not be manned in sufficient depth was one thing, but even more importantly, the whole front was never effectively covered. When the 24th Division was deployed in the area of Taejon there was a gap between its western flank and the coast of about 100km (62 miles) in which there were no friendly troops at all. To the east, the nearest ROK formation was deployed to the north of Sangju some 80km (50 miles) distant. It was therefore reasonably easy, even in difficult country, for the KPA to move unimpeded to the left or right of the UN defences.

Despite this advantage, the North Koreans, in advancing from the 38th parallel virtually to the gates of Pusan in 38 days, had achieved a remarkable feat. They still appeared to hold the initiative at the end of July, when General Walker issued orders for all his troops to withdraw behind the Naktong River, where plans had been made for his forces to occupy strong defensive positions. The river offered a good natural obstacle and it was Walker's intention finally to force the North Korean army to a halt. If the line did not hold Pusan would be lost.

2. The Pusan Perimeter

By the end of July 1950 the situation of the United Nations forces in Korea had become desperate. Reinforcements had arrived but the impetus of the North Korean drive could not be halted. Slowly but surely the UN front line had been driven back until General Walker, the commander of the UN forces in Korea, knew that defeat was inevitable unless he stopped the retreat. The enemy had to be brought up against a strong defensive position.

Before the end of the month reconnaissances had been carried out to decide on a line of defences from which to make a 'last ditch' stand, and from which, once the enemy had been held, a counter-offensive might be launched. The line

chosen formed an outer perimeter protecting the vital port of Pusan: the last town of any size remaining in UN hands and one which it was essential to protect if further urgent reinforcements and supplies were to find their way to the beleaguered UN Command.

The Pusan Perimeter, as it soon became known, formed a roughly rectangular area in the southeast corner of the Korean peninsula. In the west it was bounded by the Naktong River running south from Waegwan to where it joined the Nam River. From there the chosen line ran due south to the coast. The northern boundary ran east from Waegwan through the rugged mountains of the southern Taebaek to join the east coast at Yongdok.

From north to south the perimeter stretched for some 130km (80 miles) and from east to west approximately 80km (50 miles). The defensive positions along the Naktong River were sited on the east bank which formed a significant natural obstacle to the forces of the Korean People's Army (KPA). When covered by observed artillery, mortar fire and tactical air support it would, it was hoped, force a major delay on the enemy and, at last, blunt his lightning advance.

General Walker issued the order for all formations to withdraw behind the Naktong on 1 August in order to take up these new positions. But even as this final deployment was being carried out a new threat developed from the west. Elements

The Pusan perimeter

Kumchon
Pohang-dong
Naktong River
Yongchon
Kuryongpo-ri
Taegu
EUSAK
HQ
Kyongju
Ulsan
Naktong
Bulge
Yongsan
Samnangjin
Naktong River
Nan River
Masan
Pusan

United Nations Command
front line positions
mid Sept 1950

Left: Corporal Carroll Vogles (on left) and 1st Lieutenant Grady Vickery of the 35th Regimental Combat Team discuss the situation on the Naktong River front.

of the US 24th and 25th Divisions raced to stop the gap as the KPA made a thrust against Masan, scarcely 50km (30 miles) from Pusan itself. The swift reaction of the US troops just succeeded in stabilising the perimeter line.

The perimeter now contained approximately 47,000 US combat troops together with 45,000 men of the army of the Republic of Korea (ROK). The Naktong River line was held from the south coast to Waegwan by the US 25th Division, the 24th Division and the 1st Cavalry Division with its right flank at Waegwan. The re-formed ROK army was deployed through the mountains along the northern line with II Corps on the left joining the Americans at Waegwan and I Corps on the right stretching to the east coast. General Walker's headquarters, that both of the Eighth US Army in Korea (EUSAK) and of all the UN forces (including the ROK army, which came under his control by an agreement of 14 July), was located at Taegu, to the rear of the link-up between the US and ROK armies.

Within a few days further reinforcements began to arrive to stiffen up the defences and to provide a very necessary depth to the deployment of troops in areas thought to be particularly critical. The first to arrive was the US 29th Infantry

Below: US troops in action with a bazooka during the fighting of the summer of 1950. In the Pusan Perimeter, communist attacks were held off by solid defence, and every available method had to be used to knock out KPA tanks. Bottom: The scene at a first aid station within the perimeter at Pusan. An army padre prays as the wounded are tended.

Regiment from Okinawa, which was sent immediately to bolster forces in the Masan area in the south. The story of this regiment's arrival in Korea demonstrates just how extremely serious the UN position had become. On 15 July the regiment

was warned to be prepared to move to Korea. It was very low in numbers so the men available were reorganised into only two battalions instead of the normal three. On 20 July a draft of 400 recruits arrived in Okinawa by ship. They were issued with weapons and equipment, allocated to the two battalions, and the regiment sailed the next day. It disembarked at Pusan on 24 July and on the next afternoon found itself in the front line. Not one man had set the sights on his rifle, none of the regimental mortars had been test-fired and the newly issued machine guns were still completely clogged with protective carbon grease. The two battalions were, not surprisingly, extremely badly mauled when they first came into contact with the enemy on 27 July. After its desperate baptism of fire the 29th Regiment, or what remained of it, was incorporated into the 25th Division.

Mobilising the Marines

Other reinforcements reaching Korea at the end of July included the 5th Regimental Combat Team from Hawaii, which was also sent to the Masan area. After action there it was integrated into the 24th Division. On 31 July leading elements of the US 2nd Division began to arrive in Korea. This was the first formation to be sent to fight in Korea from the United States itself. The first regiment to disembark was dispatched to join the 24th Division while the remainder of the understrength division formed the army reserve.

An important addition to the order of battle ranged against the North Koreans arrived on 2 August in the form of the 1st Provisional Marine Brigade of the United States Marine Corps. It had been offered to General MacArthur soon after the war started and he had accepted the offer with alacrity, sensing immediately a use for the particular expertise the Marines offered. His initial plan was that the brigade would form part of an amphibious landing force which he hoped to be able to put ashore behind the enemy lines. However, the situation had become so grave that the Marines were diverted from Japan to land at Pusan to boost the forces in the perimeter.

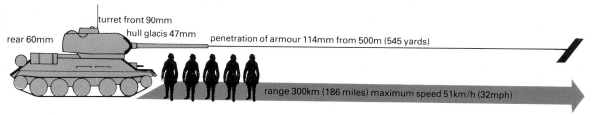

T34/85
weight 32 tonnes (31.5 tons) length 7.5m (24ft 6in) height 2.38m (7ft 10in) armament 1x85mm gun, 2x7.62mm machine guns ammunition carried 56 rounds for 85mm, 2745 rounds for machine guns

turret front 90mm
hull glacis 47mm
rear 60mm
penetration of armour 114mm from 500m (545 yards)
range 300km (186 miles) maximum speed 51km/h (32mph)

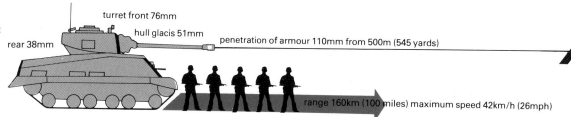

Sherman M4A3
weight 31.5 tonnes (31 tons) length 7.53m (24ft 9in) height 2.93m (9ft 7in) armament 1x76mm gun, 2x0.30in machine guns, 1x0.50in machine gun ammunition carried 89 rounds for 76mm, 7750 rounds for 0.30, 6250 rounds for 0.50

turret front 76mm
hull glacis 51mm
rear 38mm
penetration of armour 110mm from 500m (545 yards)
range 160km (100 miles) maximum speed 42km/h (26mph)

The mobilisation of the Marine Brigade was fraught with problems. It was composed of elements from Marine units serving in both the Atlantic and the Pacific, boosted by a call-up of large numbers of reservists. Most of its equipment was of World War II vintage, and had to be taken out of depots in the United States and brought up to a satisfactory state for combat. When the brigade finally sailed (from west-coast ports) there was insufficient shipping to carry all its vehicles and many were left behind.

During the voyage, news broadcasts gave details of a continual deterioration in the UN position in Korea as the front was gradually pushed back towards Pusan. Conditions on the ships were very cramped with little room for exercise or training of any sort. There were no intelligence reports available whereby the brigade could learn about the tactics and capabilities of the enemy they were about to meet. All in all, it had been a rush job. Morale in the ranks was high, but there were certainly anxieties among the senior officers of the brigade as to how the situation would develop.

On 4 August, with all his forces in position in the perimeter line, General Walker ordered all bridges over the Naktong River to be blown. The stage was now set for a last desperate effort to hold the enemy. But Walker was not content simply for his troops to conduct a static defence from prepared positions. He was, in any case, an aggressive and

Top and bottom: The M26 Pershing tank, one of the mainstays of US armoured units. Above: A comparison of the US Sherman and the T34/85. Opposite page top: Naval support was a vital aid to UN ground forces. Opposite page centre: Exhausted infantry of the US 19th Infantry Regiment in July 1950. Opposite page bottom: US observers watch the effects of an artillery barrage on communist positions.

determined man. With the arrival of additional manpower he made plans to hit back at the enemy wherever and whenever possible.

His first opportunity came in the Masan area, where he hoped to drive the enemy back and out of the town of Chinju, thus reducing the most immediate threat to Pusan itself. Using units of the 25th Division, now augmented by the 5th Regimental Combat Team and the Marine Brigade, Task Force Kean (named after the commanding general of the 25th Division) was ordered to launch a counter-offensive to retake Chinju, thereby pushing out the line of the perimeter away from Pusan. This counterstroke was set in motion on 7 August. Initially some gains were made, particularly by the Marines on the coastal flank. However, Chinju was not taken, and by 14 August Task Force Kean had withdrawn to its original start point. It had been hoped that this attack would have caused the KPA to redeploy divisions away from areas to the north but this did not happen. On the contrary, one of the reasons for calling off the offensive was the fact that the KPA 4th Division had launched an attack across the Naktong River.

Walker was fighting a desperate struggle, but he did enjoy one great advantage in his organisation of the defence – the strength of US air power, that pounded KPA positions day and night. Air strikes had covered the retreat to Pusan; and they were to assist mightily in the defence of the perimeter. Indeed, without air cover, the perimeter could hardly have been held, and the communists would have secured the whole peninsula. (For details of this air support see chapter 10.)

Having come up against the Pusan Perimeter defensive line and recognised that the UN defences were well-sited on commanding ground, the KPA High Command realised, with some alarm, that they had to break through them to reach Pusan and further that they had to do so quickly if they were to hold onto their gains. Kim Il Sung and his generals had estimated that they could maintain the momentum of their attack for up to two months and that, thereafter, the necessary reinforcements and supplies to sustain their army would be exhausted. On that basis they had until the end of August at the latest to achieve victory. The remainder of the month of August was thus to witness a series of attempts to dislodge the UN forces from their positions.

The attack against the US 24th Division in the Naktong Bulge was one of the first of these attacks. The Bulge was so named because of the wide curving sweep that the river makes just to the north of the junction with the Nam River. The Bulge measures something in the order of 8km (5 miles) from north to south and the loop itself, from east to west, approximately 6km (4 miles). The 24th Division held the line at this point and was stretched out very thinly on the ground. Small observation posts were deployed forward, overlooking the river, and to the rear the company positions often had gaps of 3km (2 miles) between them. Counter-attack forces were of course deployed in depth behind this flimsy forward screen. In addition, all likely enemy assembly areas, forming-up points, start lines and river-crossing sites were covered.

The 4th Division of the KPA was ordered to mount the attack. Its main aim was to seize and expand a bridgehead across the river and to push on rapidly eastward to take the town of Miryang. Sited as it is on the main road and rail route from Taegu to Pusan, Miryang was of critical importance to the UN forces. If they took it the North Koreans would have effectively cut the perimeter in two.

Leading elements of the KPA 4th Division commenced crossing the Naktong during the night of 5/6 August. Brushing aside the forward American outposts, the North Koreans quickly established themselves on the east side of the river. Despite that fact that it was over 400m (440yd) wide at this point, tanks and guns were quickly over the river ready to exploit the bridgehead.

General Walker recognised the seriousness of the threat and used the strongest element of his scant reserves to counter it. He put the Marine Brigade under the command of the 24th Division, with the task of launching an immediate counter-

attack. It went in on 17 August. Fierce fighting ensued and for three days the issue hung in the balance. After several initial reverses the Marines succeeded in driving the North Koreans back across the river on 19 August.

Simultaneously with the strike into the Naktong Bulge the KPA was mounting another major attack further north. Using no less than five divisions, their aim was to break through the UN lines to take Taegu, where General Walker had set up EUSAK HQ. Success here would lead them south along the main road/rail axis from Taegu to Pusan. It was just at this point in the northwest corner of the Pusan Perimeter that the ROK army joined up with EUSAK. No doubt the enemy knew this and reckoned on punching through at what they thought would be a weak point in the line where coordination of effort on the part of the UN forces would be likely to be most difficult.

The US 1st Cavalry Division on the right of EUSAK and the 1st and 6th Divisions on the left flank of the ROK army bore the brunt of several heavy actions. Three separate attacks were launched. On 5–8 August the KPA 1st and 13th Divisions crossed the Naktong and advanced southwards towards the ROK 1st and 6th Divisions. By 15 August these KPA divisions, despite initial delays, were dangerously poised some 25km

(15 miles) north of Taegu in the area of Tabu-dong. Further to the west the KPA 15th Division, moving on 5 August, crossed the Naktong with the assistance of tank fire and swept up into the high ground in the east before turning south and reaching a position some 5km (3 miles) northwest of Tabu-dong. Thus the combined forces of three divisions of the KPA were by the middle of the month positioned to advance on Taegu. General Walker made plans to reinforce the ROK 1st and 6th Divisions with US troops as and when the need arose.

Meanwhile, the KPA 3rd and 10th Divisions were assembled to the west of the Naktong opposite and slightly south of Waegwan. Both were thus opposed by the US 1st Cavalry Division. The 3rd Division made to cross the river on the

night of 8/9 August but the US troops were ready for them. Of its three regiments only one succeeded in getting across and into the hills east of the river. The other two set out to cross the river an hour after the first, by which time the US defences were fully alerted and waiting. As the North Koreans waded across the wide river in 1.5m (5ft) of water, flares and star shells burst over them and mortars and artillery opened up with an accurate and deadly fire which decimated the two regiments and forced the remnants of both to return west across the river. The regiment which had earlier crossed the river unscathed was attacked and routed on 9–10 August by units of the 1st Cavalry Division, leaving only stragglers to make their way back over the river. In these actions the KPA 3rd Division suffered terrible casualties, and it took no further part in the war until the end of August, by which time it had been brought up to strength with unwilling conscripted soldiers.

The North Koreans had intended that the KPA 10th Division should attack eastwards across the Naktong in coordination with the 3rd but it did not attempt a crossing until the night of 11/12 August. Leading elements of the division advanced to seize the high ground east of the river and succeeded in overrunning the forward positions of the 1st Cavalry Division. By 0900 hours on 12 August powerful artillery concentrations and air strikes broke the enemy and caused them to retreat back across the river.

By 14 August the level of the water in the Naktong had dropped considerably and at dawn on that day another major assault was mounted across it. Leading

elements of one division reached high ground 2km (1½ miles) east of the crossing site. By midday a large concentration of forces had assembled by the river and was preparing to cross using barges and rafts. Once more air strikes and gun and mortar fire caused major casualties to the North Koreans and brought about an early collapse of this initiative. In this fast and furious defensive action one US field artillery battalion fired so many rounds so fast that all its gun barrels suffered damage.

There still remained in the northwest sector the threat from the KPA 1st, 13th and 15th Divisions which by 15 August were concentrated ready to move on Taegu. Most of their units faced the ROK 1st Division and to increase their capacity they were issued with 21 new T34 tanks to bring tank battalions up to strength.

The Bowling Alley

To combat this threat General Walker on 14 August ordered a regiment from the 25th Division, which had just fought the enemy in the Naktong Bulge, to move northwards to the Taegu area to bolster the army reserve. By 16 August the regiment had arrived and immediately its commander was ordered to reconnoitre likely enemy approach routes to Taegu from the north through the ROK 1st Division front. The next day Walker ordered the regiment to deploy on the Tabu-dong–Sangju road to secure Taegu against attack. The road was in the ROK 1st Division area and already that division had reported an enemy unit with six tanks only 3km (2 miles) north of Tabu-dong. At last light on 17 August the regiment was deployed astride the road. It had its own artillery and mortars and a tank company (equipped with Pershing M26 tanks) was attached to it. The next day elements of a further artillery battalion were placed under its command.

On 18 August the regiment was ordered to attack northwards along the road. At the same time two regiments of the ROK 1st Division were also to attack: they were deployed in the high ground extending away from the road on each side. The advance began at 1300 hours and for the first hour nothing was encountered but a

small North Korean outpost. Then the US force was ordered to halt as the ROK regiments on its flanks had met heavy enemy resistance which had stopped their advance. The US regiment was ordered to take up defensive positions astride the road.

At this point the road was quite straight and the high ground rose steeply away from the narrow valley. The regiment deployed across the valley with four tanks positioned in the centre by the road and river and a further four tanks as a reserve held to the rear. The scene was now set for a week of tank battles in which the KPA strove to break through the US defences. Day and night they mounted attack after attack and each one was repulsed. The valley where the actions were fought came to be known as the 'Bowling Alley' after one night attack led by North Korean tanks. They used armour-piercing shells which glowed like balls of fire as they hurtled along

The great advantage that the UN forces enjoyed in Korea was superior air power. Indeed, without this advantage it is difficult to see how they could have avoided defeat in 1950. Opposite top: US Navy Sky Raiders pound communist positions with rockets. Opposite below: In spite of the relatively small threat from the North Korean air force in 1950, US troops still observed standard anti-aircraft drill, and set up light anti-aircraft artillery. Top: Infantry run for cover protected by an M26 Pershing tank, August 1950. Tanks were rarely used against each other in classic armoured engagements in this war, but they acted as very useful mobile artillery. Above: Close-quarters fighting, as US troops clear an area using a bazooka.

the length of the narrow valley towards the US tanks, as if playing a nightmarish game.

The tank battles fought for possession of the Bowling Alley during this week were, although small in scale, among the most important of the war. No less than 13 T34 tanks were positively accounted for as well as five self-propelled guns. The last North Korean attack came in the early hours of 24 August. It was a small affair compared with some of the earlier ones, and it was easily broken up. Later that same day the US regiment was ordered to break off contact with the enemy and return to the 25th Division in the south, leaving the ROK 1st Division to stand guard over the approaches to Taegu. The position on this sector of the front had, for the moment, been stabilised.

At the same time as the battle for the Naktong Bulge and the stalwart defence of Taegu, another desperate battle was raging over on the east coast. The front line running eastwards from Taegu was held by the ROK army, and the battle for the east coast port of Pohang-dong was

fought by the ROK 3rd, 8th and Capitol Divisions supported by a number of US units committed at critical moments in tactically vital sectors. Ranged against these forces were the KPA 5th, 8th and 12th Divisions plus an independent regiment.

Covering the flank

This flank of the Pusan Perimeter was seen by General Walker as extremely important. It did not cover a main axis southwards towards Pusan, but the road network was certainly capable of being used to achieve a sudden and decisive breakthrough to the port, and further, the forces covering it were far from strong. In the middle of August it seemed that such a breakthrough was about to happen.

At first the ROK army appeared to be holding onto the ground they occupied: inland from the coast they did much damage to the KPA 8th Division, virtually eliminating it from the contest. However, an independent KPA regiment made its way unchallenged southwards

Above: A recoilless rifle in action. The recoilless rifle gave infantry great punch, while remaining relatively light and portable. Right: US troops, M1 carbines hitched over their shoulders, give a wounded comrade support towards a field dressing station. Right above: Victims of the fighting in the Pusan Perimeter are buried, September 1950.

through the mountains until it reached Angang-ni, inland from Pohang-dong. Here on the night of 10/11 August US units, part of a task force sent to defend Yonil airfield, were ambushed successfully and considerable casualties were suffered. The extent of the enemy's advance was now obvious and all eyes turned to the ROK 3rd Division, which had the task of holding the narrow coastal belt to the north of Pohang-dong.

Early in August the division was holding the town of Yongdok but by 9 August it was compelled to withdraw southwards until it redeployed in defensive positions in the area of Changsa-dong. There it continued to deny the enemy the use of the main road south to Pohang-dong. On 10 August KPA units moving through the mountains cut the coastal road to the south of the 3rd Division, however, and the situation became critical. To avoid capture the division was evacuated by sea and the road to Pohang-dong lay open to the North Koreans.

Despite taking Pohang-dong it was becoming clear that the KPA divisions on this sector of the front were overstretched and that the impetus of their advance was beginning to slow down. General Walker, as commander of EUSAK, raised additional task forces to assist the ROK forces in the area. Together they managed to contain the fighting, and by 20 August Pohang-dong had been retaken and this

sector of the Pusan Perimeter was also stabilised.

The last ten days of August saw a lull in the fighting along the whole length of the front. It was, however, only a prelude to further fierce conflict. Having failed to break into the Pusan Perimeter in the complex set of battles fought throughout the early part of August the KPA High Command paused only to reorganise and re-equip their divisions, to prepare them for yet another dramatic offensive against the UN front. They attributed their failure in August to a lack of coordination of the various attacks that they launched

at that time. The UN Command had been able to respond in each area as the main thrust developed there. For this renewed offensive much planning effort was devoted to ensuring that the whole length of the perimeter was struck by KPA forces at exactly the same time.

In outline the North Korean plan was for the 6th and 7th Divisions to attack the US 25th Division in the south of the perimeter opposite Masan; the 2nd, 4th, 9th and 10th Divisions to assault through the Naktong Bulge in the US 2nd Division area; the 1st, 3rd and 13th Divisions to break through the US 1st Cavalry Division; the 8th and 15th Divisions to strike at Hayang and Yongchon to cut the UN communications between Taegu and Pohang-dong (which were held by the ROK 6th and 8th Divisions); and finally the 5th and 12th Divisions would break through the ROK Capitol and 3rd Divisions and seize Pohang-dong.

In the last week of August UN aerial reconnaissance revealed major KPA activity. Troops were on the move and assembling in concentration areas; supplies were being brought in and distributed, and there was in the western sector considerable activity on the west bank of the Naktong including, by night, the construction of underwater bridges. These were made of logs, sandbags and rocks built up to just below water-level, and were thus, in muddy water, very difficult to detect.

On the night of 31 August the North Koreans struck. In the south they quickly broke through into the rear of the US 25th Division, occupied Haman and thus directly threatened the town of Masan. Further to the north, in the US 2nd Division's area, the Naktong was crossed by strong groups of KPA forces. Units of the American division were either forced back or bypassed until the divisional front was virtually broken in two.

In the Taegu area the US 1st Cavalry Division was forced to give ground in the face of the onslaught; Waegwan was lost and the enemy were on the point of capturing Taegu itself. So dangerous did the situation appear that General Walker moved his main EUSAK HQ back out of the town to Pusan, retaining only a small tactical HQ forward, from which he fought the battle. East from Taegu the situation was no better. Deep penetrations had been made to cut the main road and rail route from Taegu to Pohang-dong and on the coast Pohang-dong itself once more fell to the KPA assault.

So critical had the situation on all sectors become by 5 September that Walker ordered his staff to draw up orders for a general withdrawal to the Davidson Line (so-called after an engineer brigadier-general who had earlier planned it on Walker's orders). During the night he discussed the possibility of withdrawal with his divisional commanders and his senior staff officers. In the event the orders were not issued and the army stayed where it was.

In the next day or two reports from all sectors indicated that the impetus of the North Korean advance was beginning to slow down. By 8 September it was certain that it had come to a halt. Walker had been right to stay where he was: the enemy was, for the time being, exhausted.

The ultimately successful UN defence of the Pusan Perimeter throughout August and early September merits further consideration. How was it that the US and ROK divisions succeeded in fighting off ferocious KPA attacks then, when earlier attempts to hold the enemy, from the time the war commenced on 25 June, had crumbled in a succession of almost un-mitigated disasters? The answer cannot be found in any one explanation.

The very speed and the extraordinary depth of the North Korean advance was in part responsible for their later failures. Any army would have been hard-pressed to provide the necessary logistic back-up behind such a lightning advance and, whereas the fighting troops of the KPA were, on the whole, well-trained and equipped, there were many weaknesses in their supply and re-equipment capabilities. When these functions were put to the test using the limited road and rail communications available, they failed. In any case the high equipment losses, especially tanks and guns, incurred during the fighting could not be made good. Some KPA formations even left their guns behind in the final September offensive because they had no ammunition for them and knew that none would be available.

Pershings and rocket-launchers

In contrast General Walker found that once he had established the final Pusan Perimeter along the Naktong River line he had no major supply problems. The distance from Pusan to any point on the perimeter was very short, nowhere longer than 120km (75 miles). And supplies of both men and material to the UN forces were to increase rather than diminish as the days went by.

A major advantage enjoyed by the KPA in the early stages of the war was also denied them once the perimeter had been established. No longer was it possible to use the outflanking tactics that had achieved such devastating results. From early August Walker's forces were more easily able to cover the whole front line in greater numbers and thus each unit and formation was sited to provide support for its neighbour in the event of an attack. To break through in these circumstances the North Koreans were forced to engage in direct frontal assaults and such was the strength of the UN line, sited in excellent defensive positions, that only limited and local successes were achieved.

By August the capability of the UN forces was also immeasurably enhanced by the arrival of ever-increasing supplies of technically superior weapons. Pershing tanks were found to be a match for the T34/85s of the KPA, and 3.5in rocket-launchers gave a far greater anti-tank capability to the infantry. The ability of the UN forces to put down witheringly effective artillery and mortar fire on the

Opposite page top: US troops take a break from the action. Above: A member of the 5th Regimental Combat Team which saw some of the hardest fighting at Pusan.
Top: The breakout from Pusan.
Triumphant US troops display a captured communist flag.

North Korean infantry frequently broke up attacks even before the enemy reached the forward UN positions. These weapons were used to particularly good effect during the battles for the Bowling Alley.

Despite these advantages the battles might still not have been won but for the leadership demonstrated by General Walker. He had proved himself an outstanding commander in northwest Europe during World War II when the Allies were on the offensive; here, in Korea, he was faced with a totally different situation. A seemingly unstoppable enemy army gave every indication that it intended to drive him and his men into the sea. His problem was threefold: how to slow down an almost uncontrolled withdrawal; how to stabilise the situation; and how to turn it round to his own advantage.

He was an aggressive man by nature and consequently not popular in the US Army. In Korea he virtually bullied his generals into submitting to his will. At times it appears they were more apprehensive of facing him than the enemy. He even said to one general that he did not want to see him back from the front again unless it was in a coffin! His light-

ning visits to command posts, and his knack of always turning up at the crucial moment, no doubt helped to instil a more determined attitude into his subordinate commanders – which in turn filtered down to the men in the front line.

Not that Walker's overbearing and bullying attitude was his sole contribution to the successful defence of the perimeter. He demonstrated a quite remarkable flexibility and agility of mind in his reaction to successive crises. He moved his forces from sector to sector along the front line with bewildering speed, stopping a gap in his defences or counterattacking where he sensed enemy weakness.

As August turned to September, slowly but surely the morale of the UN forces began to rise. They were gradually wresting the initiative back from the KPA. However, what really encouraged the UN Command in Korea was the knowledge of the impending counterstroke being planned against the North Koreans. General MacArthur's daring plan for an amphibious landing at Inchon, designed to cut off the KPA's lifeline well behind the front, was about to be launched.

3. Inchon

To put the Inchon landing of 15 September 1950 in its proper perspective it has to be borne in mind that the planning and preparation for it were taking place at a time when reports coming out of Korea told only of unmitigated disaster for the United Nations forces there. It is this background situation which singles out the decision to land at Inchon as one of unparallelled audacity and which puts it in a category of its own even when compared with amphibious landings conducted in the Pacific, the Mediterranean and northwest Europe during World War II.

Throughout World War II the techniques of amphibious warfare had been developed to an unprecedented level, and amphibious landings had been used many times to speed up offensive operations by causing the enemy to divert troops to counter new threats from unexpected quarters and further to demoralise an enemy already on the defensive. General Douglas MacArthur had won for himself a great reputation during the war for executing such ship-to-shore operations with outstanding success. Now, as Commander-in-Chief, UN Command, he demonstrated an extraordinary courage and an even greater strategic insight in initiating the planning of such an operation at a time when his troops already committed to the battle in Korea appeared to be having difficulty in arresting the continuing progress of the enemy.

By the time the operation actually went in (on 15 September 1950), it seemed a natural, sensible development and one likely to bring the war to a rapid close. However, during the planning of the operation, from early July when MacArthur first considered an amphibious landing up to the end of the first week of September when the UN forces were battling to hold the Pusan Perimeter, there had always been a very real possibility that the UN forces in the peninsula might be driven into the sea.

On 28 June, three days after the war started, MacArthur had paid a flying visit to Korea to see the situation for himself. He returned to his HQ in Japan with two thoughts uppermost in his mind: the first, quite clear and specific, was that US forces must be committed immediately to the land battle in Korea; the second, only just beginning to take form, was that the best way to seize the initiative from the North Koreans, however successfully their attack continued in the weeks ahead, would be to execute an amphibious landing in their rear and take them by surprise.

In pursuance of this latter idea he told his chief of staff in Tokyo, General Edward Almond, to consider possible alternative plans for such a seaborne attack aimed to strike at the enemy communications in the area of Seoul. For MacArthur there was never any doubt that Seoul should be the target of such an operation. Besides being of strategic importance in that all north–south road and rail links passed through the city, it was of great political significance as the capital city of the Republic of Korea (ROK).

On 4 July a conference of senior US Army, Navy and Air Force representatives was called in Tokyo. The aim of the conference was to consider the implications of an amphibious assault behind the enemy lines. By this date elements of the US 24th Division were in Korea with the rest of the division on the way to join them, and a second division of the US occupation forces in Japan, the US 25th Division, was under warning to move as well. As discussions at the conference progressed, MacArthur indicated that he wanted the US 1st Cavalry Division to be used in the amphibious assault, leaving one remaining US division in Japan. The outcome of the conference was the decision to mount a major landing operation by 1st Cavalry Division on or around 22 July. The operation was given the codename 'Bluehearts'. In order to provide the division with amphibious ex-

pertise a US Marine Corps officer was attached to the divisional HQ staff.

Planning for the landing went ahead immediately with a great sense of urgency, tinged in places with not a little scepticism. While the idea was brilliant, and might, in theory, change the outcome of the war, the period of 18 days between the start of planning and the date of the landing was scarcely realistic. It was, after all, a generally accepted rule inherited from World War II that a divisional-scale landing would require a minimum of 60 days to plan and prepare; and this with all the necessary resources available within the theatre of war. On 4 July there were scarcely any ships or craft of the type needed in either Korean or Japanese harbours, nor for that matter sufficient specialist units or personnel to mount such an operation.

In the event the planning of the landing was cut short when on 10 July it was

General Douglas MacArthur (above, seated) was the mastermind behind the audacious landings at Inchon. MacArthur had faced great difficulties in getting the plan accepted, for Inchon was far from ideal as the target for amphibious operations. Nevertheless, he had his way, and the results fully justified his gamble. Among the senior commanders who had an important role to play in the operation were (above, standing left to right), Brigadier-General E. K. Wright, Rear-Admiral J. H. Doyle and Major-General E. M. Almond. Opposite page: Lieutenant-General Lemuel C. Shepherd, Commander Fleet Marine Force Pacific, on board the USS Mount McKinley in Inchon Bay. Left: The Marines who went ashore at Inchon were under the direct command of Major-General Oliver P. Smith, here photographed on the day of the landings, 15 September.

decided to abandon the operation owing to the increasingly desperate situation developing in the front line in Korea. Despite the arrival of the first American troops, the UN forces were still fast falling back under relentless North Korean pressure. As far as MacArthur was concerned, however, although circumstances had demanded that Operation Bluehearts be ruled out, he was far from giving up the concept of an amphibious landing. He had to accept the re-deployment of the 1st Cavalry Division to reinforce the UN forces already in the peninsula, but this to him simply meant he would have to lay his hands on more troops to achieve his aim.

The same day that Operation Bluehearts was cancelled he had a meeting with Lieutenant-General Lemuel Shepherd of the US Marine Corps, recently appointed to command the Fleet Marine Force Pacific. Together they formulated a dispatch to the Joint Chiefs of Staff (JCS) requesting that the Provisional Marine Brigade already authorised for service in Korea be augmented by two further regiments to form the 1st US Marine Division, to be placed at Mac-

Top: Landing craft make for the shore at Inchon. Above right: A Vought Corsair, one of the mainstays of US naval aviation during the final years of World War II, flies above the invasion fleet. Right: US Marines head for Blue Beach at Inchon, in the tracked landing vehicles that had been developed for the campaigns in the Pacific Islands in World War II.

Arthur's disposal. This would mean that MacArthur would have a division available already conversant with amphibious warfare and able to spearhead his envisaged counterstroke.

Debates and discussion

Also on 10 July, MacArthur learned that earlier demands for troops from the United States had been agreed and that the 2nd Infantry Division was under orders to prepare to move to Korea. His request for the use of the 1st Marine Divi-

sion was not to be so readily granted, however. The JCS were fearful of reducing Marine forces elsewhere in the world in case the Soviet Union should take advantage of any weakness to act in Europe. This meant that to meet MacArthur's demand men of the Marine Corps Reserve would have to be mobilised and President Truman was loath, for political reasons, to initiate this step.

The continued deterioration of the situation, paradoxically, came in the end to serve MacArthur's purpose, and on 20 July the JCS confirmed to him that he could have another Marine regiment, but not before November. A further fierce exchange of dispatches between MacArthur and the JCS followed and the former finally got agreement for the Marines to be available for use by mid-September. It was not, though, until 10 August that the JCS agreed to let him have the third Marine regiment which would bring the division up to war strength.

Meanwhile planning for a landing went ahead even after Bluehearts had been cancelled. Before the Korean War had broken out MacArthur had established at his Far East Command HQ in Tokyo a Joint Strategic Plans and Operations Group (JSPOG). This organisation was given the task of formulating plans for a new amphibious landing to replace Bluehearts. On 23 July Brigadier-General Edwin Wright, head of JSPOG, put forward three alternative suggestions for a landing: at Inchon; at Kunsan, also on the west coast; or at Chumunjin on the east coast.

MacArthur had always preferred Inchon, however, largely because of its proximity to Seoul, and he ordered that detailed planning for Operation Chromite, as the landing was now codenamed, should go ahead on the basis that the landings would go in there on 15 September. On 12 August MacArthur's Tokyo HQ issued the first written confirmation of his decision to go for a major amphibious landing at Inchon with the aim of seizing Seoul. Many arguments and discussions were still to come but at least MacArthur's mind was made up.

As planning moved ahead it was decided that the landing would require the combined forces of two divisions, and the 1st Marine Division and the 7th Infantry Division were earmarked for the task. On 26 August X Corps HQ was inaugurated to command and control the force. There was some argument as to who should command the corps, made up, as it was, of both Marines and US Army men. The navy and the Marines argued that the Commander Fleet Marine Force Pacific had a great deal of experience in amphibious warfare and should be the obvious choice. However, as was so often the case, MacArthur had the last word. He decided that his chief of staff at Far East Command, General Edward Almond, should command the corps. MacArthur saw the appointment as totally logical: Almond had been at the centre of planning since the war began and was available immediately to oversee the preparations for the operation. The way MacArthur saw it, the operation would lead to a swift end to the war and then Almond would revert to his former appointment as chief of staff.

The composition of the landing force had been decided but it was one thing for the units to be listed on paper and quite another for them to be physically assembled. While preparations for the landing went ahead frantic efforts were made to produce the personnel and material to bring the two divisions into being.

The 1st Marine Corps Division would be made up of the 1st Marine, the 5th Marine and the 7th Marine Regiments. Of these the 5th Marines were already fighting in the Pusan Perimeter as the 1st Provisional Marine Brigade. They would have to be extricated from the front line in order to join the division for the landing. The decision as to the date of their release from General Walker's Eighth US

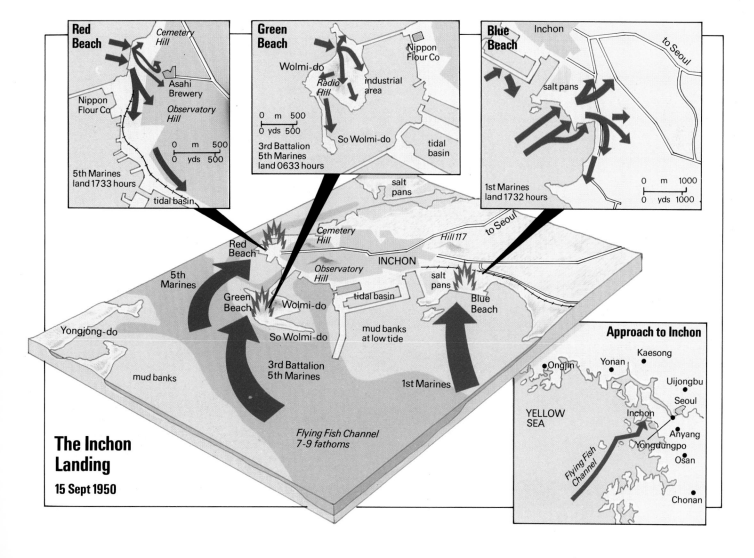

Red Beach — Cemetery Hill · Asahi Brewery · Nippon Flour Co · Observatory Hill · 5th Marines land 1733 hours · tidal basin · 0 m 500 · 0 yds 500

Green Beach — Wolmi-do · Nippon Flour Co · Radio Hill · industrial area · So Wolmi-do · tidal basin · 0 m 500 · 0 yds 500 · 3rd Battalion 5th Marines land 0633 hours

Blue Beach — Inchon · to Seoul · salt pans · 1st Marines land 1732 hours · 0 m 1000 · 0 yds 1000

Cemetery Hill · Red Beach · 5th Marines · Green Beach · Wolmi-do · So Wolmi-do · 3rd Battalion 5th Marines · Yongjong-do · mud banks · Observatory Hill · INCHON · tidal basin · mud banks at low tide · Flying Fish Channel 7-9 fathoms · Hill 117 · to Seoul · salt pans · Blue Beach · 1st Marines

The Inchon Landing
15 Sept 1950

Approach to Inchon — Ongjin · Yonan · Kaesong · Uijongbu · Seoul · YELLOW SEA · Inchon · Anyang · Yongdungpo · Osan · Flying Fish Channel · Chonan

Army in Korea (EUSAK) was highly controversial. The Marines were, as Walker saw it, totally necessary to defend Pusan and he could not do without them. The navy and Marines were equally adamant, refusing point-blank to mount the Inchon landing without them. General Almond attempted to find a compromise but failed, and finally MacArthur ruled in his favour. The 5th Marines were extricated from the front line on the night of 5/6 September and moved back to Pusan where they began immediate preparations for Inchon.

The 1st Marines were the second Marine regiment to be ordered to Korea. They had been made up to war strength following the call-up of reservists: the best of them going to the 1st Marines while others took the place of serving Marines in other units. Thus a number of experienced and well-trained men were released to mingle in the 1st Marines with those returning from civilian life.

Together with the Divisional HQ and other units the 1st Marines sailed from the United States to arrive in Japan between 22 August and 6 September. Time was running out, and the third regiment, the 7th Marines, which was only authorised to be formed on 10 August, was put together in great haste with officers and men being gathered together from the far corners of the world. Most came from the United States but some were with the Fleet Marine Force Atlantic and one whole battalion was at sea in the Mediterranean. It was transported to Korea via the Suez Canal and arrived at Pusan on 9 September without the slightest idea what its task would be. It joined the rest of the regiment, which had reached Japan between 28 August and 6 September.

Half-strength division

The second division designated for the operation, the 7th Infantry Division, was the last of the four original US divisions making up the occupation force in Japan. As each of the other divisions had prepared to move to Korea shortages of manpower had been made up by taking men from the 7th Division. In July the division had lost no less than 140 officers and 1500 men in this way. At the end of the month, when it was ordered to prepare for action in Korea, it stood at less than half strength. To make up in part for this shortfall the entire infantry reinforcement arriving in the Far East between 23 August and 3 September was posted to the division. It also received all artillery reinforcements for an even longer period. Still the numbers were far short of what was needed and a unique method of boosting the divisional strength was then employed.

General MacArthur requested General Walker to recruit and send to Japan suitable young South Korean men to be armed and equipped and then assimilated into units within the division; as many as a hundred to each company and battery. These men, known as 'Katusa' (Korean Augmentation to US Army), arrived in Japan only just in time: they were quickly allotted to units as the last preparations were being made to embark for the landing. Only a few of these strange recruits could speak English, but most problems

Origin of forces

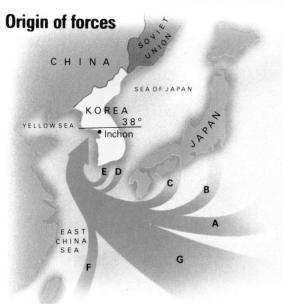

A 1st US Marine
   Division from USA
B 7th US Infantry
   Division from Japan
C 30 LSTs from Japan
D 5th Regiment 1st US
   Marines from Pusan
   Perimeter
E Troops from South
   Korea
F 7th Regiment US
   Marines of Sixth Fleet
   from Mediterranean
G 230 ships from
   navies of USA,
   Great Britain,
   Australia, Canada,
   New Zealand, South
   Korea, France

were overcome by employing the 'buddy system', whereby an American soldier worked together with one or two Koreans in his section.

Even though MacArthur was set on landing at Inchon a great deal of controversy centred on this choice. Opposition to the use of this particular port area stemmed largely from the US Navy, supported by top-level Marine Corps generals. The JCS in Washington were also far from convinced that it was the best place. There were very good reasons for this anxiety because physically the port of Inchon presented a large number of problems which would have to be overcome for the assault to be successful. In the words of one officer experienced in amphibious warfare: 'We drew up a list of every conceivable and natural handicap – and Inchon had 'em all.'

At about 10m (32ft) the tidal range in Inchon harbour is one of the biggest in the world: at high tide the water laps against the sea walls of the harbour and at the low point the water retreats into narrow shallow channels in between which large

Left: US Marines storm into action at Inchon, taking the sea wall in their stride. Surprise and the speed of the operation ensured that US casualties were low. Right: The ordered confusion of the beaches after the landing as supplies pour in.

expanses of mud flats are exposed. Inevitably, with such a tidal range the water ebbs and flows extremely rapidly, creating serious difficulties for ships and small craft attempting to negotiate the tortuous twists and turns of the swiftly flowing currents in the deeper channels.

The depth of water against the sea walls at high tide was cause for further anxieties. Because of the gradient of the seabed close to the shore a Tank Landing Ship (LST) would require a high tide of at least 9m (29ft) to get in to unload. Such tides were rare and in the period envisaged for the operation would only occur on 15 September and then again on 11 October. The date already selected, 15 September,

could thus not be changed except by a month, should other factors demand it. The exact timing of the high tides was also a crucial factor. The morning high tide on that day was at 0659 hours and the evening tide reached its maximum at 1919 hours.

Amphibious assaults in World War II had taught the planners that open beaches of a particular gradient provided the best conditions for getting men, vehicles and equipment ashore and, further, that a beachhead could best be secured to allow for deployment inland if the landing took place in reasonably open country. At Inchon neither of these conditions prevailed. To make matters even worse, if the ultimate objective for the landing lay in the seizure of the capital, Seoul, then there remained the major obstacle provided by the Han River before the city could be entered.

As planners grappled with these problems the undercurrent of anxiety and outright opposition from the naval side mounted until it became clear that a showdown would be necessary. It was thus decided that there should be a top-level conference at MacArthur's HQ in Tokyo on 23 August. This date coincided with a visit by two members of the JCS, General Lawton Collins, US Army Chief of Staff, and Admiral Forrest P. Sherman, Chief of Naval Operations.

The meeting commenced at 1730 hours and apart from the two representatives of the JCS and General MacArthur and his senior staff officers there were a number of other senior officers present. General MacArthur opened the conference with a few words and then Brigadier-General Wright explained the plan in general outline. There then followed a series of briefings by naval and Marine experts in all aspects of amphibious warfare. All the problems were brought out into the open.

Landing with the tide

The point was made that because of the tidal range the landings would have to be made at high tide to allow the Tank Landing Craft and other craft to get to the beach. The two high tides of 15 September were just after first light and just before last light. As amphibious craft in large numbers could not negotiate the narrow harbour approaches in the dark the landing would of necessity be in the evening and darkness would fall just at the moment when the Marines would be seeking to deploy inland.

Another problem highlighted at the briefing centred on the narrowness of the shipping channels into the harbour. It would only take one naval fire-support ship to run aground in the approaches and no other ships would be able to get into the harbour at all.

It was also considered highly risky to make a landing against a sea wall rather than onto a beach. The problem for the assault troops would be immense and there would be grave difficulties experienced in clearing routes for tanks, guns and vehicles leaving the landing points. To make matters worse, no sooner were the leading waves of assault troops ashore than they would be in the town, with its buildings and streets which were so easy for the North Koreans to defend.

At the end of what could at best be considered a pessimistic assessment of the difficulties confronting the landing force and at worst an outright condemnation of MacArthur's very personal choice of Inchon, the two chiefs of staff sought clarification on one or two points of detail and, more seriously, questioned the possibility of alternative sites further south along the west coast. Then it was Mac-

Arthur's turn. He spoke for 45 minutes without recourse to notes. He pointed out that virtually all the enemy's forces were closely engaged in trying to break through the Pusan Perimeter. The KPA had very few units deployed in the rear, even in the Seoul area, where their supreme HQ was installed. Their lines of communication were over-extended and all replenishment passed through the road and rail bottleneck at Seoul. Once these were cut the KPA offensive would instantly collapse. He also stressed the great moral effect that the capture of so important a city as Seoul would have on the UN forces and, even more important, on the Korean people themselves.

He recognised that the landing was a gamble but stressed that there were many

Above left: After the landings, MacArthur was able to go ashore in triumph. Here, his caravan of jeeps stops for a moment on the road to Seoul, opposite two knocked-out KPA tanks. Above: Disconsolate KPA prisoners taken during the Inchon landings. Left: US troops form up before moving out of Inchon town. Opposite page top: The battle for Seoul. By the time the UN forces moved onto the South Korean capital, the KPA had recovered from its initial surprise and the fighting was far more intense than in Inchon itself.

factors supporting his choice of Inchon. The enemy, too, knew the difficulties of landing there; indeed, they might well discount the possibility of an attack against Inchon because of them. In this way surprise would be achieved and success made very likely. To illustrate his point he sought a historical precedent by alluding to Wolfe's 'impossible' scheme to take Quebec in 1759. Turning to the question of alternative landing sites he dismissed them as not offering the opportunity instantly to sever the North Korean main supply routes.

The green light

Doubts may still have existed in some minds after this momentous conference but, however reluctantly, the chiefs of staff had been won over. On 28 August they sent a dispatch to MacArthur signifying their approval for the operation, and the stage was finally set. The frantic planning and preparation continued in a race against time. The composition of the naval force was confirmed as were detailed timings of the moves from Japanese ports and out of Pusan harbour. Deficiencies in assault craft and vessels were remedied by vigorous and imaginative action. It was, for example, calculated that 57 LSTs would be needed and the navy could only muster 17 throughout the Far East. These were assembled and the remaining 40 were commandeered from the Japanese to whom they had been given after the war to operate a rudimentary ferry system between the islands. They came complete with Japanese crews.

Intelligence agencies were hard at work attempting to gain information on the enemy forces in the Inchon–Seoul area. On 4 September it was estimated that there was a total of approximately 6500 KPA soldiers in the general area, of which some 2500 were likely to be protecting the Inchon port complex and town. Aerial reconnaissance was flown at frequent intervals to ascertain changes in enemy deployments and many naval parties were sent ashore to confirm navigation channels, hazards to shipping and the presence of mines in the approaches to the harbour.

One particular venture captured the

imagination of all who heard about it. A US naval lieutenant on the JSPOG staff, Eugene F. Clark, landed from a British destroyer with a small party of men on the island of Yonghung-do about 25km (15 miles) out to sea at the mouth of the Flying Fish Channel leading to the inner harbour. From friendly Koreans from the fishing village on the island he obtained a great deal of information to update that already in the hands of the planners. He was able to confirm details of the main navigation channels into the harbour; the state of the muddy beaches below the sea walls (he found them too soft to be of any use); and even the height of the sea walls themselves. Some of his informants made sorties into Inchon and the surrounding countryside to bring back confirmation of enemy unit strengths and positions. All these details were sent by radio back to the planners in Tokyo and disseminated to the units involved in the landing. In the end, the enemy discovered his whereabouts and on 14 September he left the island for another, Palmi-do, on which stood the main beacon light signalling the entrance to Inchon harbour. That night he got the beacon to work so that it could be used by the naval force arriving for the landing.

Everything was done to maintain secrecy over the Inchon landing until the last possible moment. Decoy landing groups went ashore at many other places along the coast; aerial reconnaissance was carried out in detail over many other areas apart from Inchon; and air and naval bombardments were similarly directed at other targets along both the west and east coasts. Diversionary landings, too, were planned and executed to keep the enemy constantly in a state of uncertainty as to the intentions of the UN forces. Eventually, of course, all attempts to disguise the landing site would have to be abandoned as the necessary preliminary naval bombardments and air-to-ground attacks went in to soften up the target areas prior to the landing itself. It took a fine sense of judgement to decide on the optimum duration of these attacks: they had to be short enough to keep the enemy guessing until the very last possible moment but long enough to ensure the neutralisation of likely threats to the landing forces.

The plan for the landing itself on 15 September was worked out to the last possible detail. The main assault was to take place on the evening tide, thus allowing ships and craft to make their way to the beaches up the difficult channels in daylight. The small island of Wolmi-do posed a problem, however. It lay just off Inchon itself and was linked to it by a causeway. Aerial and ground reconnaissance (by Lieutenant Clark's men) had located major enemy defences on the island and it was clear that it would constitute a major threat to landings at Inchon if it was not neutralised beforehand. It was decided therefore that a landing on Wolmi-do would have to be made on the early morning tide of 15 September to secure it prior to the arrival of the main forces.

The final plan in outline was for a battalion landing team from the 5th Marines to land in the morning on Wolmi-do (Green Beach) and for the remainder of the 5th Marines to land at Inchon north of Wolmi-do causeway (Red Beach) in the evening. Simultaneously with the 5th Marines' landing, the 1st Marines would land on a beach (Blue Beach) to the south of the town close to some salt pans. The initial aim for both the 1st and 5th Marines was to establish their beachheads that evening. Early next morning they were to push out, link up with each other and then move inland, seeking to capture Kempo airfield quickly and to cross the

Han River and enter Seoul.

The organisation of the fleet to carry the landing forces and provide them with support throughout the operation was a task of enormous complexity. The timetabling of sailings was intricate, as ships were setting out from several different ports. To complicate matters even more, as ships were being loaded at Kobe in Japan a typhoon struck the area. Loading had to be halted for 36 hours, several ships broke their moorings and some equipment was damaged. Despite these setbacks all was eventually prepared, and the various convoys, according to their role and the speed of individual ships, commenced sailing for Inchon from 10 September.

Typhoon in the Tsushima Strait

Many groups of ships were already at sea and some were in the final stages of embarkation when a second typhoon moved towards the Tsushima Strait. Its movement indicated that it would hit the seas in which the major part of the task force would be sailing on 12/13 September and it looked set to cause sufficient delay to prevent the force landing on the critical day of the 15th. By judicious alteration of timings and routes the centre of the storm

was avoided, and it passed without causing major damage. Ships struggled to maintain course and position through mountainous seas and the fiercest of winds while below decks the men of the Marines lay totally prostrate from seasickness. By 14 September the worst was over and the fleet in its correct order was approaching the Flying Fish Channel leading to Inchon.

For some days the preliminary bombardment from sea and air had been in progress. From 4 September air attacks had been carried out against targets in the area of Seoul and Inchon with the aim of isolating the latter and preventing full use of routes into the area by enemy reinforcements after the landing had gone in. US Marine Corps aircraft next attacked the island of Wolmi-do on a massive scale using napalm, with the intention of clearing undergrowth and thus exposing the KPA positions on the island.

By 13 September the ships of the US Navy and the British Royal Navy that made up the Gunfire Support Group had arrived off Inchon. The four cruisers of the group remained 13–16km (8–10 miles) offshore while the six destroyers entered the Flying Fish Channel. As they moved into position opposite Wolmi-do an enemy minefield was seen, partially

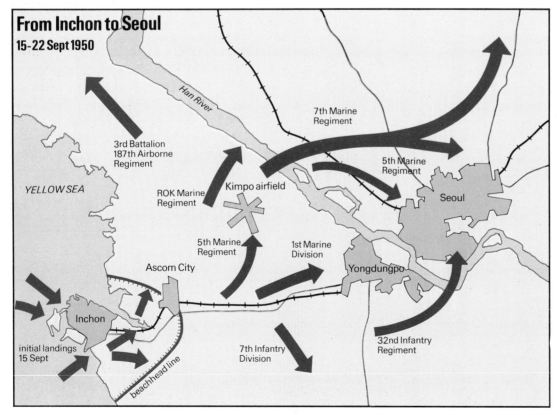

From Inchon to Seoul
15–22 Sept 1950

Han River

7th Marine Regiment

3rd Battalion 187th Airborne Regiment

YELLOW SEA

ROK Marine Regiment

Kimpo airfield

5th Marine Regiment

Seoul

5th Marine Regiment

1st Marine Division

Ascom City

Yongdungpo

Inchon

initial landings 15 Sept

beachhead line

7th Infantry Division

32nd Infantry Regiment

Opposite page top left: A North Korean is captured by UN forces, and searched by a US soldier while a South Korean covers the prisoner. Opposite page top right: The 16-in guns of the USS Missouri *open up on a target on the Korean mainland. Opposite page bottom: The cruiser USS* Toledo *pounds away during the preliminary bombardment of the west coast of the Korean peninsula in the weeks preceding the Inchon landings. In order not to give away the site of the landings, large stretches of the coast were exposed to naval gunfire.*

exposed by low water. Some of the mines were exploded by automatic fire but the anxiety remained that there might be more in the channel the destroyers were using.

Just after 1230 hours the destroyers opened fire on Wolmi-do, the closest from a range of approximately 1200m (1300 yd). For an hour and a quarter they put a heavy barrage down on the island. The ships made such inviting targets standing in so close to the shore that the North Koreans put their 76mm guns on the island into action against them. Some superficial damage was done to the destroyers but by disclosing their positions the enemy guns made themselves sitting targets and most were knocked out by the naval gunners. The signal for the destroyers to withdraw came at 1347 hours and they weighed anchor and made best possible speed away and out to sea. They had sailed in on the ebb but the tide had turned as they left and pointed their bows seawards, conveniently eliminating the need for complicated manoeuvres in the narrow channel.

Next came the cruisers' turn: from 1352 hours for an hour and a half they put down a shattering barrage of fire onto the island with their 6in and 8in guns. Both destroyers and cruisers were covered throughout their missions by carrier-based aircraft which also attacked Wolmi-

do. As dusk came on the whole Gunfire Support Group made out to sea to wait for morning.

The next day, 14 September, the whole programme was repeated, though some ships shifted their barrages to selected targets in Inchon. When the group withdrew in the afternoon it was reported that the enemy defences on Wolmi-do were virtually completely destroyed. As one Marine pilot said, the island was 'one worthless piece of real estate'.

At midnight that night the ships carrying the force due to land at Green Beach in the morning made a perfect rendezvous

with the Gunfire Support Group. Then, after a brief pause, the new arrivals weighed anchor and, ship by ship, made their way towards Flying Fish Channel en route for Wolmi-do. The final confirmation for L-Hour (the time of the landing) at 0630 hours was signalled round the fleet and then at 0520 hours came the order for embarkation into the landing craft. By 0540 hours the Landing Craft Vehicles and Personnel (LCVP) were circling at the rendezvous point 1·6km (1 mile) from the shore prior to heading for the beach. Suddenly the destroyers and cruisers opened fire simultaneously

on Wolmi-do, and the whole island was for a moment covered in sheets of flame and billowing smoke. This bombardment was escalated into a veritable inferno at 0615 hours when three rocket ships fired their salvos one after the other straight at the island, two aimed at the beach where the Marines would land a few minutes later and one at the reverse slopes of the island's two hill features where KPA reserves might be grouped. Lastly, 38 Marine Corps Vought F4U Corsairs flew in low over the landing craft to give them cover during the last few vital minutes before they hit the beach.

At 0633 hours the landing craft carrying two companies of the 3rd Battalion, 5th Marines reached the beach. The right-hand company had the task, after clearing the beach, of wheeling to the right and storming up Radio Hill, the most prominent feature on the island. There was scarcely any sign of enemy troops and the company reached its objective by 0655 hours, just after the 3rd Battalion HQ group landed on the beach. The left-hand company, with the objective of taking North Point and crossing the island to secure the causeway from Inchon, also met little resistance initially. A team laid a belt of mines across the causeway to defend it against counter-attack from the mainland and then the company cleared the enemy from the totally destroyed oil refinery to the south of where the causeway joined the island.

A section of six tanks landed soon after the first infantry companies and then the reserve company came in. The latter's task was to secure the high ground to the north of the island and though the ground had been covered by the first company ashore it was here that the only sign of organised resistance occurred. North Koreans coming out of their dugouts after the bombardment eased off opened fire and lobbed grenades at the Americans. The tanks were called up and the threat was quickly neutralised.

At 0800 hours the battalion commander radioed back to the seaborne HQ that the island was secure. He then reorganised his three companies in defensive positions and everyone settled down to wait. The tide went out and the battalion lay marooned throughout the day until the main landing against Inchon scheduled for approximately 1730 hours in the evening.

The capture of the island had been, for the Marines, a relatively simple affair. They had lost no-one and only suffered 17 men wounded. First estimates showed that 108 enemy soldiers had been killed and 136 captured, while a number who refused to surrender had been buried alive by tanks fitted with bulldozer blades in the caves in which they chose to remain.

With the capture of Wolmi-do the enemy in Inchon was fully alerted and it was to be expected that attempts would be made to reinforce the town, which was obviously about to come under attack. With this in mind, carrier-based aircraft flew sorties throughout the day within a 40km (25-mile) radius of the landing area in an attempt to seal off the town and harbour. At the same time, using the navigable channels that remained at low tide, assault shipping was manoeuvred into position ready for the main landing.

The main naval bombardment of Red and Blue Beaches commenced at 1430 hours and shortly afterwards the order was issued to prepare the landing force. The men of the 1st and 5th Marines, minus the battalion of the 5th already on Wolmi-do, went over the side of their transport ships and into the landing craft. It was then confirmed that the landing was to go in at 1730 hours as planned.

The main aim of the 5th Marines, landing on Red Beach just north of the Wolmi-do causeway, was to storm into the town itself and seize Cemetery Hill and Observatory Hill: features which dominated the whole of the town and the immediate countryside around. The 1st Marines, landing south of the town on Blue Beach, had the job of pressing on inland behind the town and cutting off the main road running from Seoul into Inchon.

As the first wave of landing craft broke from circling in the rendezvous area and headed for shore the rocket ships loosed off some 2000 rockets at the two beaches, and aircraft went in low over them to strafe the enemy. So low and so perfectly timed was their attack that empty cannon shells fell into some of the landing craft just as they approached the beach. The 5th Marines had the added advantage of fire support provided up to the last second by the weapons of the 3rd Battalion on Wolmi-do. The men on the island were given a grandstand view of their comrades as they hit Red Beach.

The men of the 1st and 2nd Battalions of the 5th ran onto the beach at 1733 hours. Scaling ladders were used in most cases to scale the sea walls and get ashore, though some craft steered into gaps in the wall which had been opened up by the gunfire that had preceded their arrival. For the most part the resistance from the KPA, shattered by the bombardment, was limited in strength and came only from small groups of men. On the left of the landing area a larger group, well dug-in, was more tenacious, and the Marines lost eight men killed before the North Koreans were dislodged. Notwithstanding this minor setback, by 1755 hours Cemetery Hill had been taken and, on the right, the leading company was moving forward through the town towards Observatory Hill. Gathering darkness slowed down this advance and yet the hill had been occupied by midnight.

The landing at Blue Beach did not run quite so smoothly. As the leading wave of landing craft headed for the landing site their problem was all too obvious. Ahead of them lay a thick pall of smoke which totally obscured the shoreline. Many fires had been started in Inchon by the preliminary bombardment and as the fires spread so did the billowing smoke which, caught by the wind, drifted southwards into the Blue Beach area. Visibility was made even worse by the gathering rainclouds.

Hitting the beaches

The first three waves of craft made it to the beach through the choking banks of smoke but thereafter considerable confusion set in. Few tractors or craft had serviceable compasses so the helmsmen steered more by instinct than accurate reckoning as they ploughed into the thickening gloom. Groups of craft were split up and command elements divorced from the fighting men. Almost the whole of the reserve battalion landed completely in the wrong place some 2000m (2200yd) from the designated beach area.

Despite great confusion made even greater as night fell, the leading battalions were eventually reorganised and, moving out from the beach, they managed to reach their designated objectives in the early hours of the morning of 16 September. The main road from Seoul was reported cut at 0130 hours. It must, however, be pointed out that the 1st Marines were very fortunate indeed not to meet determined enemy resistance.

Scarcely had the 5th Marines cleared Red Beach than the final landing of the

Left: US infantry, supported by M46 tanks, on the advance. Below: KPA troops captured on the first day of the Inchon landing by the US 1st Marine Division await transfer to prison camps. Below right: Three infantrymen, all from Los Angeles, set up their Browning .30-inch water-cooled machine gun just southwest of Inchon during the expansion of the bridgehead there. The Browning had first come into service shortly after World War I, and was an extremely dependable weapon.

day took place. In order to provide vehicles, ammunition, food, water and fuel for the division to press on the next day, eight LSTs followed the assault troops onto Red Beach where they ground up against the crumbling sea wall, side by side, almost touching. There then followed a night of feverish, frantic effort as the stores were unloaded in a race against the tide: the empty vessels had to leave on the morning tide to allow a further eight LSTs to take their place with equally vital stores for the follow-up operations.

Despite many minor setbacks and not a few mistakes, perhaps inevitable with an amphibious landing, the Inchon landings were an undoubted success. The bulk of the 1st Marine Division went ashore and established a firm beachhead from which to advance towards the Han River and the ultimate goal, Seoul. Thanks to the small number of enemy stationed in the area, made the weaker during the preliminary supporting bombardments, the opposition on the beaches and inland was only intermittent and the Marines suffered very few casualties: in all, 20 men killed, one missing in action and 174 wounded.

Soon after dawn on 16 September the 1st and 5th Marines linked up and thereby successfully created the beachhead perimeter with Inchon inside it. ROK Marines were given the task of restoring order in the city, leaving the Marine Division to concentrate on their advance eastwards. During the morning a column of T34 tanks was observed advancing with infantry down the main road from Seoul. Marine aircraft were sent against the column and two separate attacks were put in, effectively neutralising it.

The Marine regiments progressed inland against only sporadic opposition. The axis of advance was the Inchon–Seoul road, with the 5th Marines to the north of it and the 1st on it and to the south. By last light on 16 September they had covered sufficient ground to put the beaches out of range of enemy artillery fire, and by 1800 hours Major-General Smith, the divisional commander, had established his HQ ashore and assumed command of land operations.

Both Marine regiments occupied defensive positions on the night of 16/17 September. At dawn a forward position of the 5th Marines observed a column of six tanks with supporting infantry advancing towards their foxholes. Lying low, they allowed the enemy to drive into their positions without disclosing their presence. Suddenly, at a range of only 70m (75yd), Pershing tanks and rocket-launchers opened fire on the North Koreans, catching them completely by surprise. Within five minutes all the tanks had been destroyed and the accompanying infantry killed, taken prisoner or put to flight. Shortly after this action General MacArthur, soon ashore after the landing, inspected the ambush site with his staff.

The 5th Marines advanced rapidly throughout 17 September and by nightfall had seized the southern half of Kimpo airfield. Repulsing several counter-attacks that night the regiment occupied the whole of this major airfield complex soon after first light next morning. (Aircraft were flying from the field on 20 September, only five days after the first troops were ashore.) Pressing on relentlessly, the 5th had, by last light on 19 September, occupied the whole of the

south bank of the Han River which lay within their sector of the front.

To the south of the Seoul–Inchon road the 1st Marines advanced eastwards more slowly. Their frontage was wider and the ground over which they fought was a great deal more rugged. They were also responsible for the road itself and the settlements astride it. Clearing these was a slow and dangerous business. On 17 September the regiment came up against a regiment of the KPA 18th Division hastening forward in an attempt to delay the Marine advance. The Marines kept going, however, and slowly but surely progress was made. On 19 September enemy mines slowed the advance once more, but by nightfall leading elements of the 1st Marines were poised on the outskirts of Yongdungpo, the southern suburb of Seoul and the only part of the city south of the Han River.

Battle for Seoul

At this point two regiments of the US 7th Infantry Division, the 31st and 32nd Infantry, relieved the 1st Marines, and the 7th Division took over responsibility for the front line from the main road southwards. The arrival of this division allowed the 1st Marines to sidestep to the left and fill the gap created by the northeasterly movement of the 5th Marines as they took Kimpo airfield prior to crossing the Han River.

For the next three days the 1st Marines fought desperately to take Yongdungpo, which was defended in considerable strength. A daring exploit by a company of Marines who entered the city almost by mistake and unnoticed by the North Koreans served to bring the battle to a close, and by the evening of 23 September the 1st Marines were poised to cross the Han River and enter Seoul proper.

Once the 7th Division was in position its task was to hold the line south from Yongdungpo and to advance rapidly to cut off the main routes towards Seoul from the south, thereby preventing reinforcements reaching the city from the bulk of the KPA forces deployed in the south against the Pusan Perimeter. After some occasionally fierce fighting in which both sides used tanks, the division found

itself by 23 September firmly in position astride these vital routes.

Meanwhile, having reached the Han River in the northern sector on 19 September, the 5th Marines, scarcely pausing for breath, went straight into an assault crossing of the river. They made their first attempt that night but suffered a setback. The next morning, using a variety of crossing equipment – ferries, amphibious tractors and boats – they were successful. Despite frequent stiff resistance they forced their way eastwards until they paused on 21 September on the outskirts of Seoul with only a line of low hills between them and the city.

The KPA now deployed in the greatest strength it could muster to defend the capital city. The 5th Marines fought to enter the built-up area through the hills from the west but were held up by tenacious enemy groups which made them fight for every inch of the way. To ease the pressure on the 5th Marines the 1st crossed the Han River from the Yongdungpo area on 24 September. The two regiments linked up but still they made little or no progress. Every attack was countered by fierce, desperate North Korean attacks using tanks and infantry.

General Almond, commanding X Corps, now endeavoured to coordinate an assault by both the Marine and the Infantry Divisions, together with ROK units. The ROK forces crossed the Han on 25 September and together the whole

body of troops struggled to overcome the stalwart enemy resistance.

Just before nightfall on 25 September an aerial reconnaissance mission reported that KPA troops were leaving the city, heading northwards, and for a moment it seemed that Seoul had fallen. Bitter fighting was to continue, however, as although the bulk of the KPA forces in the city were withdrawing, units were left behind to fight a desperate rearguard action. Fighting behind a succession of street barricades, they exacted a heavy toll among the ranks of the UN forces for every metre of territory they yielded. Against such bitter resistance it took the UN forces three days to gain complete control of the town, which they did on 28 September.

In the end the Inchon landing paid off handsomely. Organised with incredible speed and amid a great deal of controversy, the daring venture was to justify MacArthur's faith in it. The mistakes in the early stages of the landing were fortunately compensated for by a lack of ability on the part of the North Koreans. While the fighting for and in Inchon was never to lead to anxiety for the success of the operation, there is no doubt that the struggle later on as the US and South Korean troops tried to enter Seoul was as desperate as any at any time during the war. It is hard to believe that such a decisive and hard-fought action took only 13 days to complete.

4. China steps in

By the third week in September 1950 it was clear to General Douglas MacArthur that the collapse of the Korean People's Army (KPA) was at hand. His master-stroke at Inchon had turned the war around: Seoul had been recaptured and the forces in the Pusan Perimeter had managed to break out. By 8 September, Walker's men had already fought the KPA troops opposite them to a standstill and after the landings at Inchon were able to take the offensive. Attacks along the east coast and across the Naktong River took the Eighth Army rapidly north, to link up with the forces which had landed at Inchon on 26 September.

MacArthur made a case to the US Joint Chiefs of Staff (JCS) that stopping at the 38th parallel would leave the military and political situation unresolved, whereas a successful drive into the North would unite Korea under a single government and give it a defensible natural boundary with China along the Yalu River.

An aura of infallibility had settled on MacArthur since Inchon, and the JCS dutifully pressed his arguments on President Truman. MacArthur, however, was more than a national commander. He was not only Commander-in-Chief, US Far East Command, he was also Commander-in-Chief, United Nations Command. The crossing of the parallel would require UN endorsement. Radio Peking was crackling with warnings that China would come into the war if North Korea were invaded. There were conflicting views at the United Nations, and appre-hensions that the Soviet Union might enter the war.

After days of agonising delay caused by the need to get political and diplomatic consensus, the JCS on 27 September authorised MacArthur to proceed:

> Your military objective is the destruc-tion of the North Korean armed forces. In attaining this objective you are auth-orized to conduct military operations, including amphibious and airborne landings or ground operations north of the 38th Parallel in Korea, provided that at the time of such operations there has been no entry into North Korea by major Soviet or Chinese Communist Forces, no announcement of intended entry, nor a threat to counter our operations militarily in North Korea. Under no circumstances, however, will your forces cross the Manchurian or USSR borders of Korea . . .

The first part of the JCS directive reflec-ted MacArthur's own recommendations; the second part included the caveats needed to get approval.

Lieutenant-General Walton H. Walker (Bulldog to his troops and the press, Johnny to his friends), commander of the Eighth US Army in Korea (EUSAK) then breaking out of the Pusan Perimeter, presumed that Major-General Edward M. Almond's independent X Corps would come under his command now that Seoul was taken and the forces joined. Walker's staff was working up plans to send X Corps north to take Pyongyang, the ancient capital of Korea. But MacArthur did not find it necessary to consult with Walker; he had already decided on his next move. No uniformed person pre-sumed to argue with MacArthur; not his strongest field commanders and certainly

Left: US infantrymen, with some protection against the cold (mittens, caps with ear-flaps) prepare to meet a communist attack. They are armed with the standard M1 rifle. The sergeant on the left has a weapon with a flash suppressor fitted to the muzzle. Below left: Trudging through the snow, US infantry advance in the wake of M4A3 Sherman tanks. In the mountainous terrain through which the Chinese were to launch many of their attacks, armoured support was impossible.

not his sycophantic staff at Far East Command in Tokyo. Even the JCS – chaired by Omar Bradley and with J. Lawton Collins for the army, Forrest P. Sherman for the navy, and Hoyt S. Vandenberg for the air force – were deferential, even obsequious, toward the great man.

Crossing the parallel

MacArthur replied to the JCS on 28 September with a brief outline of his plans. The Eighth Army would attack across the 38th parallel to seize Pyongyang. The still-independent X Corps would land at Wonsan in a great amphibious envelopment and then march overland to join the Eighth Army. The newly arrived US 3rd Infantry Division would remain in reserve at general headquarters (GHQ) in Japan. Only Republic of Korea (ROK) forces would operate north of the line Chongju–Yongwon–Hungnam.

The JCS came back with its approval the next day, 29 September, the same day that General MacArthur escorted President Syngman Rhee in his triumphal return to his capital, Seoul. On the following day MacArthur broadcast his ultimatum calling for North Korean unconditional surrender, otherwise: 'The early and total defeat and complete destruction of the North Korean armed forces and war-making potential is now inevitable.'

Launching such a great offensive would require a considerable logistical build-up. The ports at Pusan and Inchon were already taxed to capacity. But not much resistance was anticipated. It was estimated that of the 165,000 North Koreans who had invaded the South not more than

25,000 to 30,000 had found their way back to North Korea and that there were not more than 30,000 to 50,000 KPA troops in various states of training.

As September ended, the UN Command numbered about 315,000. Nearly 200,000 of these were in the ground combat forces, of which half were American and half South Korean. All five of the US Army divisions had large numbers of 'Katusa' (Korean Augmentation to US Army) to fill out their understrength ranks. Altogether there were over 22,000 Katusa, for the most part half-trained or untrained recruits, loosely integrated with the Americans under the 'buddy system' or in small units. Many observers felt that the scheme was not a great success. The British 27th Brigade, with 1700 troops, was also present, as was the 1300-strong Philippine Battalion Combat Team.

The Eighth Army's cumulative casualties since the beginning of the war totalled 24,172 at this point – 5145 killed in action, 16,461 wounded in action (of whom 422 died of wounds), 402 reported captured, and 2164 missing, many of whom were prisoners-of-war.

Air power

Three elements of Lieutenant-General George E. Stratemeyer's Far East Air Forces (FEAF) that had already provided essential air cover in all theatres of the war would support the forthcoming offensive. Major-General Earle E. 'Pat' Partridge's Fifth Air Force was to maintain air superiority and give close support, with priority to go to the Eighth Army. Almond's X Corps had its own private tactical air force in the form of the 1st Marine Aircraft Wing and would also be supported by the navy's carrier-based Task Force 77. Major-General William H. Tunner's Combat Cargo Command would continue to provide airlift and aerial evacuation of casualties and Major-General Emmett 'Rosy' O'Donnell's Bomber Command would continue its area bombardment.

On the eastern front, the ROK I Corps, commanded by Brigadier-General Kim Baik Yil and nominally still part of the Eighth Army, had moved up the coast with its 3rd and Capitol Divisions. The

3rd Division, on President Rhee's direct orders, stole a march on the Eighth Army, crossed the parallel on 1 October and took the small North Korean port of Yangyang the day after.

In Inchon harbour, on board his flagship the cruiser Rochester, Vice-Admiral Arthur D. Struble reactivated Joint Task Force Seven for the amphibious operation to land X Corps at Wonsan. He was worried about mines. He had been Commander Mine Force Pacific at the end of World War II and he knew that the shallow and muddy coastal waters of the Sea of Japan were ideal for mine warfare. Already, on 26 September, the destroyer Brush had struck a mine while shelling a shore battery on Korea's northeast coast and with 13 dead and 34 wounded barely made it to Sasebo, Japan, for repairs. On

the 30th the destroyer Mansfield had struck a contact mine while searching for the aircrew of a downed Douglas B-26 Invader. On 1 October the wooden-hulled minesweeper Merganser was sunk by a floating mine north of Pohang. It had to be assumed that the approaches to Wonsan were mined. Struble ordered all Seventh Fleet minesweepers under way for Wonsan.

Before the break-out from the Pusan Perimeter Walker had divided his Eighth Army into two corps commands. As a break-out force he grouped together as I Corps, commanded by Major-General Frank W. Milburn, the US 1st Cavalry Division and 24th Infantry Division, the British 27th Infantry Brigade, and the ROK 1st Division. The newly activated IX Corps, lacking in signal troops, was

Below left: During its retreat north, the KPA was harried unmercifully by the US air forces, with raids on communications and installations making the task of keeping the retreating army together very difficult. Here, B-26 medium bombers have completed a strike. Right: The landings at Wonsan complemented those at Inchon. There were certain problems at Wonsan, however, due to the mines that had been laid, and the South Korean minesweeper in this photograph was one victim. Below right: The rigours of the Korean winter were a great shock to the US forces, many of whom were poorly equipped to face such cold.

under the command of Major-General John B. Coulter and given control of the US 2nd and 25th Divisions. It was to follow behind with responsibility for mop-up operations.

On 7 October the General Assembly of the United Nations voted its explicit approval, by way of a resolution, of the crossing of the 38th parallel. Wasting no time, on 7 October Milburn's I Corps relieved Almond's X Corps north of Seoul. MacArthur's favourite division, the 1st Cavalry under Major-General Hubert R. Gay, was in the lead. Gay sent patrols across the 38th parallel on the 7th, and on the 9th the division moved up to the parallel, taking Kaesong, and beginning its fight northward. Meanwhile, Almond's two divisions went their separate ways en route to Wonsan. Major-General Oliver P. Smith's 1st Marine Division motor-marched to Inchon to embark on amphibious shipping, while Major-General David G. Barr's 7th Infantry Division moved south by rail and road to Pusan for embarkation.

On 9 October 1950, the JCS authorised MacArthur to engage Chinese forces in Korea 'as long as, in your judgement, action by forces now under your control offers a reasonable chance of success'. This directive showed a significant change from that of 27 September to MacArthur which had authorised his operations in North Korea provided that there was no action by major Soviet or Chinese com-

Left: Chinese infantry in training. The Chinese army that entered the Korean War was an experienced and resourceful foe, and most of the troops had had some kind of combat experience during the civil war between nationalists and communists in China. Below: US troops root out KPA troops operating behind the lines. Right: Dropping supplies to advancing UN troops from a C-119 transport.

munist forces. The extent of operations by UN Command was now left to MacArthur alone. There was thus no question that he was authorised to advance into North Korea; what was at issue following the retreat from North Korea in December 1950 was his judgement and competence in directing the full-scale advance to the Yalu River.

On the east coast, on 10 October, the ROK I Corps fought its way into Wonsan, 180km (110 miles) north of the 38th parallel, against heavy artillery fire and with some street fighting, thus removing the need for an amphibious assault. Walker, after flying to Wonsan to appraise the situation, proposed to MacArthur that ROK I Corps link up with ROK II Corps, which was the right flank of the Eighth Army's main body, once Pyongyang was taken. MacArthur vetoed the proposal, brusquely informing Walker that once the Marines were ashore at Wonsan he was taking ROK I Corps away from the Eighth Army and putting it under Almond's X Corps.

Minesweeper Squadron Three arrived off Wonsan from Sasebo on 10 October, to clear the way for the Marines. D-day had first been set for 15 October. There were only five days to do the sweeping, and the extent of the minefield was unknown. On 12 October the steel-hulled *Pirate* was broken in two by a mine. Her sister minesweeper *Pledge* went to her rescue, got caught in the 'cabbage patch', and was also lost, making a total of 92 casualties. A massive field of 3000 mines had been laid under the supervision of

Soviet experts. The Advance Force Commander sent a calamitous message to the Chief of Naval Operations: 'The US Navy has lost command of the sea in Korean waters . . . .'

On 15 October MacArthur had his famous meeting with President Truman at Wake Island, during which he assured the president that although the Chinese had about 300,000 men in Manchuria not more than 50,000 to 60,000 could get across the Yalu River in the face of American air power. On his return to Tokyo, MacArthur issued new orders to the UN Command. The Eighth Army and X

Corps, instead of converging along the Pyongyang–Wonsan line, would continue to operate separately, driving north to a new line roughly 80km (50 miles) south of the Yalu. Beyond that – in grudging consideration of State Department fears of the consequences if US troops were used too close to the border – only ROK troops would operate, except on MacArthur's own direct orders.

On the Eighth Army's front, elements of the KPA 19th and 27th Divisions had clung stubbornly to a ridgeline position 25km (15 miles) north of Kaesong until outflanked by the 1st Cavalry Division in

a fight that came to be known as the 'Battle for Kumchon Pocket'. To the right of the 1st Cavalry Division, Major-General Paik Sun Yup's ROK 1st Division was making spectacular progress, reaching Suan, 65km (40 miles) southeast of Pyongyang, on 16 October. Paik's foot infantry looked likely to reach North Korea's capital before Gay's motorised troopers. Walker urged Milburn to get on with it. Milburn, in turn, ordered Major-General John H. Church's 24th Infantry Division to move up on the left of the 1st Cavalry Division. It was expected that the North Koreans would make a stand on the heights in front of Sariwon. Milburn told Gay and Church that whichever division reached Sariwon first would have the honour of leading the corps attack against Pyongyang itself.

The British 27th Brigade – now the 27th British Commonwealth Brigade since the joining of the 3rd Battalion, Royal Australian Regiment on 3 October – passed through the US 7th Cavalry on 17 October and took Sariwon while the 7th Cavalry looped around to catch the enemy in the rear. The 1st Cavalry Division, by virtue of having the British 27th Brigade attached to it, thus won the right to lead the attack against Pyongyang itself. The Eighth Army's Intelligence credited the city with being defended by 8000 troops from the KPA 32nd and 17th Divisions. At the approach of the UN forces, Kim Il Sung, North Korea's premier, fled his capital after exhorting its defenders to hold it to the last man.

General Gay ordered the 7th Cavalry, Custer's old regiment, to resume the advance at daybreak on 18 October. While Milburn, the corps commander, watched from an apple orchard by the side of the road, the 3rd Battalion, 7th Cavalry, supported by 20 tanks, crashed through a dug-in reinforced battalion at Hukkyo-ri, halfway to Pyongyang. Next day the 5th Cavalry passed through the 7th and entered the North Korean capital. Almost simultaneously the ROK 1st Division came into the city from the northeast. Despite Kim Il Sung's exhortations, the capital was undefended except for scattered snipers.

The paras go in

Brigadier-General Frank S. Bowen's elite 187th Airborne Regimental Combat Team, in GHQ reserve, had arrived at Kimpo airfield outside Seoul. MacArthur ordered a jump north of Pyongyang. Delayed by rain, the 187th Airborne RCT got off from Kimpo at about noon on 20 October, lifted by Combat Cargo Command's Fairchild C-119 Flying Boxcars and Douglas C-47 Skytrains. The jump went ahead at 1400 hours, with 71 C-119s and 40 C-47s delivering 2860 paratroopers and 300 tonnes of equipment into drop zones near Suchon and Sunchon, about 50km (31 miles) north of Pyongyang. MacArthur watched the jump from his personal aircraft. There was moderate resistance. A second jump went in the next morning with 40 C-119s delivering 1093 more troopers and 100 tonnes more gear. (On that day, 21 October, MacArthur flew into Pyongyang to visit Walker and Stratemeyer. F Company,

5th Cavalry, was drawn up as a guard of honour. MacArthur asked all troopers who had been with the company since it had first landed in Korea three months earlier to take one pace forward. Only five men responded.) Next day the 1st Cavalry Division linked up with the 187th Airborne. An estimated 6000 North Koreans had been caught in the trap. A total of 2764 were dead, and over 3000 were taken prisoner.

There was a chill in the air. The brief autumn was almost over. In the hills the weather was turning bitterly cold. On 24 October MacArthur issued new orders abolishing all restraints: 'All field commanders are enjoined to drive forward with all speed and with full utilization of all forces.' The race to the Yalu was on. The ROK 1st Division followed US tanks into Kunuri on 22 October and then turned left down the valley of the Chongchon, taking a bridge site at Anju. The British 27th Brigade arrived in Sinanju on the heels of the ROK 1st Division and crossed the Chongchon River at Anju on the 24th. The approach of US I Corps toward Sinuiju near the Yalu's mouth forced Kim Il Sung to abandon that provisional capital and move inland to Kanggye in the high north central mountains. To the right of US I Corps, ROK II Corps sent its 6th Division to Huichon on the Chongchon while its 8th Division, coming along more slowly, reached Tokchon. ROK II Corps was now in extremely mountainous terrain, the forbidding Taebaek Range. Far to their right, elements of the ROK Capitol Division had taken Iwon, a minor port 120km (75 miles) northeast of Hungnam.

However, things were going much more slowly with US X Corps, sorely trying the patience of the impetuous Major-General Almond.

Not until the evening of 25 October could it be reported that Wonsan had a channel swept clear of mines. Fifteen days had been required to complete what had been expected to be a five-day sweep. Major-General Oliver Smith's 1st Marine Division landed on the beach the next morning and found its aviation counterpart, the 1st Marine Aircraft Wing, already operating Vought F4U Corsairs from the airfield. The day before the landing Smith was advised by Almond that as a consequence of MacArthur's orders of 24 October the mission of the Marines had changed. Two Marine regiments were to relieve ROK I Corps in the vicinity of Hamhung and Hungnam

and prepare for a march through the mountains to the Yalu River, while ROK I Corps moved along the coast to the far northeastern tip of North Korea. Smith's third regiment was to remain in the Wonsan area, cleaning up the remnants of the KPA 15th Division, until the arrival of the US 3rd Infantry Division.

Reaching the Yalu

The same day as the Marines' landing at Wonsan, elements of the ROK 7th Regiment, 6th Division, II Corps reached the Yalu near Chosan. Their moment of triumph would be brief. The day before, 100km (60 miles) to the south, a battalion of the ROK 2nd Regiment, 6th Division, was destroyed in an ambush near Onjong by what were at first thought to be North Koreans. That night troops of the Chinese People's Volunteers, or the Chinese Communist Forces (CCF) as they were called by the UN Command, completed the destruction of the ROK 2nd Regiment. Press reports that 20,000 Chinese had entered North Korea were denied by GHQ at Tokyo, which stated that there was no confirmation of anything more than a few Chinese 'volunteers'. The ROK 10th and 19th Regiments attempted to reach Onjong and on 29 October were themselves badly defeated, losing all their vehicles and artillery. The ROK 7th Regiment, alone in the north, tried to fight its way back. Fewer than a

Opposite page top: The USS Gunston Hall *heads for the landing area at Wonsan.* Left: *An aerial view of the landing beaches at Wonsan on 26 October, as landing craft stream onto the Korean coast.* Top: *'Amphtracks', the amphibious tracked vehicles that gave the first wave of landed troops a certain amount of mobile protection.* Above: *The UN landings at Wonsan on 26 October were being answered on the communist side by the gradual build-up of Chinese forces, here seen crossing the Yalu River. They were to make a decisive impact in the last months of 1950.*

thousand reached Kunuri, where Major-General Yu Jae Hung, commanding general, ROK II Corps, was attempting to form a defensive line. The ROK 6th Division was finished. The 8th Division took positions just north of Kunuri while the 7th Division dug in to the northeast; the Chongchon River lay between them.

The Chinese began their attack against Kunuri on the morning of 31 October, sweeping away the ROK 8th Division and exposing the right flank of Milburn's US I Corps. Milburn flew to the ROK II Corps command post, where Major-General Yu told him that all he had left were three battalions of his 7th Division. By now there were indications that the enemy was the CCF 38th and 40th Armies.

The US 8th Cavalry Regiment was at Unsan, some 30km (19 miles) north of Kunuri, and to their right was the ROK 1st Division which had faced east to cover the exposed flank. Milburn returned from his meeting with Yu and ordered the 8th Cavalry and ROK 15th Regiment to withdraw from Unsan, but it was too late. As darkness came on that evening, the US cavalrymen heard for the first time the wild sound of Chinese bugles and the shrilling of whistles. The Chinese came at them from behind a mortar bombardment and a ripple of Katyusha rockets. The 5th Cavalry Regiment was dispatched to reinforce the surrounded 8th Cavalry, but the Chinese, in a deep penetration, had already cut the road. The Chinese hurled themselves into the Americans, whether they were in prepared positions or in stalled columns of vehicles, shooting, throwing grenades, tossing satchel charges, and always there were the bugles. The 8th Cavalry, badly mauled, began falling back early on 2 November, and was ambushed by the same force that had cut the road. The troopers took to the hills, singly or in small groups. Some got around the ambush. Many were captured. Altogether the regiment lost half its strength and most of its vehicles and equipment. The enemy was identified as the CCF 39th Army.

Walker ordered a general withdrawal of the Eighth Army to the Chongchon River. The Chinese broke off their violent attack as suddenly as it had begun. On 9 November, MacArthur informed the JCS that complete victory was still possible, since the UN Command was sufficiently strong to destroy all enemy

The Chinese intervention
Nov 1950 – Jan 1951

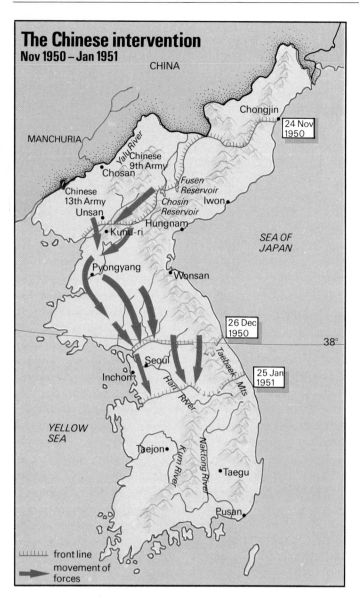

Map labels:
CHINA
MANCHURIA
Chongjin
24 Nov 1950
Yalu River
Chinese 9th Army
Chosan
Fusen Reservoir
Chinese 13th Army
Unsan
Chosin Reservoir
Iwon
Kunu-ri
Hungnam
Pyongyang
Wonsan
SEA OF JAPAN
26 Dec 1950
38°
Seoul
25 Jan 1951
Inchon
Han River
Taebaek Mts
YELLOW SEA
Taejon
Kum River
Naktong River
Taegu
Pusan

front line
movement of forces

Top: Chinese troops pose gleefully with US prisoners. Opposite page top: Chu Teh, one of the leading Chinese generals. Opposite page bottom: Chinese infantry; their flexible tactics and personal bravery surprised the UN Command. Above: UN infantry brave the biting cold.

forces then in North Korea, and US air power would prevent the Chinese from crossing the Yalu in decisive numbers. He was still optimistic.

The Eighth Army gathered its strength to renew the offensive. Walker brought forward Major-General John Coulter's IX Corps. During late October and early November, the British 29th Brigade, the Turkish Brigade, and a battalion each from Thailand, the Netherlands, and Canada, arrived in South Korea and joined the Eighth Army.

Across the mountains to the east things seemed to be going well for Almond's X Corps. Not needed at Wonsan, Major-General David Barr's 7th Division made an unopposed landing at Iwon, to the northeast, on 29 October. The 17th Regimental Combat Team was first ashore,

and was put on a one-way mountain road to Hyesanjin, 160km (100 miles) away on the Yalu. The winter winds had begun blowing out of Manchuria. While the 17th RCT marched against increasing cold to the Yalu, Barr was to send another regiment west to Fusen Reservoir, part of the hydroelectric system that fed power to Manchuria. They were to take but not damage the facility.

The advance to Chosin

The mission of the 1st Marine Division parallelled that of the 7th Division. The Marines were to advance northwest of Hungnam along a mountain road to Chosin Reservoir, site of another important hydroelectric plant, and then north to the Yalu. The 7th Marine Regiment

moved out of Hungnam on 2 November, relieved the ROK 26th Regiment at Sudong-ni, and before midnight was in heavy contact with the CCF 124th Division. The fight went uphill, through the tortuous Funchilin Pass, to a high wind-swept plateau. The 124th broke contact on 7 November and on 10 November the Marines entered the village of Koto-ri.

In Tokyo, MacArthur's press officers clung to the threadbare explanation that the Chinese were 'volunteers', which was exactly the same story as was coming out of Peking. But by 6 November, MacArthur was forced to admit to the JCS that 'Men and material are pouring across all bridges over the Yalu from Manchuria.' He asked for authority to destroy the bridges and got qualified approval: US bombers could take out the

North Korean halves of the bridges, but could not violate Chinese territory or airspace. Nor could US fighter escorts pursue communist interceptors into Manchuria. He did get permission to fire-bomb North Korea's remaining cities, including Sinuiju, which is just across the Yalu from the major Chinese air base at Antung.

A maximum air effort was mounted and on 18 November MacArthur reported to the JCS that 'The air attack of the last ten days has been largely successful in isolating the battle area from added reinforcement.' This optimistic report was only marginally accurate. O'Donnell's Bomber Command and Rear-Admiral Edward C. Ewen's Task Force 77 had developed great proficiency in bridge-busting and fire-bombing but there were new problems: heavy and increasingly sophisticated anti-aircraft fire

and a new generation of MiG fighters flying from sanctuary airfields across the border. The combined air force and navy effort cut half the bridges across the Yalu and damaged most of the rest, but the effort was increasingly costly and the effect not lasting. The Chinese threw pontoon bridges across at critical sites and the winter was freezing the river so solidly that foot soldiers could walk across. Japanese railway engineers told FEAF intelligence officers that they had once laid a railway track across the frozen Yalu.

Indeed, by the end of October, General Lin Piao's Field Army, consisting of the 38th, 39th, 40th and 42nd Armies, had already crossed the Yalu and marched, mostly at night, down the mountain spine of North Korea. Lin Piao had detached the 42nd Army to protect his flank from X Corps until General Chen Yi's Third Field Army, with the 20th, 26th, and 27th Armies, could get into position. Each numbered army had three divisions of about 8000 men each, and totalled, with HQ troops, about 30,000 men – equal to a US corps. The Chinese were a foot army, almost invisible to aerial reconnaissance. Each man was almost self-sufficient, carrying a week's supply of rice, millet and soya bean in a cotton cloth tube and enough ammunition for four or five days of violent action.

Lin Piao's attack had been a probe, not

the beginning of a major offensive, and it had yielded him some valuable lessons. Not so with Walker and MacArthur, each of whom from his own perspective, the frozen rice paddies of Korea or the Olympian heights of GHQ in Tokyo, grossly underestimated Chinese capabilities. As he got ready to resume the offensive, Walker calculated that he would be able to put 135,000 troops against an estimated communist force of 95,000, of whom 55,000 were believed to be Chinese. This underestimated Lin Piao's strength by at least half.

On the morning of 24 November MacArthur flew in his new Lockheed Constellation to Eighth Army HQ at Sinanju. Here, with Walker and Milburn, he watched the jump-off of the UN offensive that was expected to end the war. At this proud moment, Walker's Eighth Army, from left to right on line, consisted of Milburn's I Corps with the US 24th Division, the British Commonwealth 27th Brigade, and the ROK 1st Division; Coulter's IX Corps with the US 2nd and 25th Divisions and the Turkish Brigade; and ROK II Corps with the ROK 6th, 7th, and 8th Divisions, miraculously reassembled after their rout of three weeks earlier. In reserve was the US 1st Cavalry Division, the damage done to it at Unsan now patched up. With satisfaction, MacArthur announced that the war would be won in two weeks

and the Eighth Army would spend Christmas in Japan.

To complete Walker's offensive, MacArthur had ordered Almond to attack to the west to squeeze the communists between the Eighth Army and the still-independent X Corps. Almond had moved his command post from Wonsan to Hungnam on 11 November. The 7th Marines entered Hagaru at the southern end of Chosin Reservoir on 13 November. Almond planned to move his command post to Hagaru and army engineers and signal troops arrived to begin construction. The right flank of ROK I Corps was 130km (80 miles) to the west. Almond's three columns had diverged like the ribs of an extended fan. The 17th RCT from Barr's 7th Division reached Hyesanjin on the Yalu River on 20 November. On the east coast itself ROK I Corps still raced toward the north-eastern extremity of North Korea, on the border with Soviet Russia.

On 24 November, as the Eighth Army jumped off, Almond informed Smith that the 1st Marine Division was to be the northern arm of a giant pincer of which the Eighth Army was to be the southern arm. H-hour was to be 0800 hours on 27 November. By the morning of the 27th, Smith had two of his regiments, the 5th and 7th Marines, at Yudam-ni, north of Hagaru, in an attack position. His remaining infantry regiment, the 1st Marines, he had deployed by battalion at Chinhung-ni at the foot of Funchilin Pass, and at Koto-ri and Hagaru on the high plateau, so as to keep his lines of communication open back to Hungnam.

In the west, the Eighth Army's 'Home-by-Christmas' offensive went well for the first two days. Then on 26 November Chinese bugles were heard across the front. Lin Piao, holding the US I and IX Corps in place with strong secondary attacks, made his main effort, in a repetition of his late October offensive, against the still shaky ROK II Corps, driving it from the key position of Tokchong. By noon on 27 November, Walker was reporting to MacArthur that he estimated there were 200,000 Chinese in front of him, that ROK II Corps had been swept away, and that IX Corps was falling back to cover its exposed flank.

On the same day the 1st Marine Division at Yudam-ni launched an unenthusiastic attack to the west. The lead regiment advanced 2km (1½ miles) and was stopped. That night it snowed and the temperature went down to –29°C. The Chinese commander, Sung Shih-lun, had eight Chinese divisions from Chen Yi's Third Army with which to destroy the 1st Marine Division. On the night of 27 November he used three of them to attack the 5th and 7th Marines at Yudam-ni and two other divisions to attack the Marine battalions at Hagaru and Koto-ri.

On the 28th MacArthur did an uncharacteristic thing: he called Walker and Almond back to Tokyo for a secret council of war. They talked most of the night. After listening to the doleful reports of his two principal field commanders, MacArthur ordered a switch from the offensive to the defensive. Walker thought that he could hold in the vicinity of Pyongyang. Almond was still sanguine enough to believe that the attack of the 1st Marine Division to the west could succeed.

Vice-Admiral C. Turner Joy, Commander Naval Forces Far East, had his own apprehensions. On 28 November he alerted Rear-Admiral James H. Doyle, as commander of the amphibious force, to prepare for the redeployment of UN forces out of North Korea. On 30 November all ships of Doyle's Task Force 90 were ordered under way for Korea.

While the leaders talked in Tokyo, Smith, at Hagaru, took matters in his own hands. He ordered the 5th Marines to hold at Yudam-ni and the 7th Marines to open the road back to Hagaru. Hagaru, with its airstrip, had to be held, but there was not much more than a battalion there to hold it. On the 29th, the remnants of Task Force Faith, two US Army battalions from the 7th Division, came in from the east side of the reservoir, adding about 300 combat soldiers. Another reinforcement, called Task Force Drysdale after its Royal Marine commander, Lieutenant-Colonel Douglas S. Drysdale,

Above: The retreat from Chosin was a bitter blow to the US troops involved. They had been expecting total victory by Christmas, and yet found themselves in a perilous, exposed position in which retreat and then evacuation were the only courses of action. Right: A US private gratefully snatches some food. Opposite page top: The Chinese were far better prepared to deal with the Korean winter than their US counterparts. Opposite page bottom: Supplies are dropped to the troops pulling back from Chosin.

was formed at Koto-ri of a mixture of Royal Marines, US Marines, and US soldiers. It was ambushed and the column cut to pieces. The survivors reached Hagaru about midnight on the 29th.

To the west, Major-General Lawrence B. Keiser's US 2nd Division, heavily supported by the Fifth Air Force, had become the rearguard for the retreating Eighth Army. The Turkish Brigade, under Brigadier-General Tashin Yasci, was ordered to hold Wawon, east of Kunuri, to cover Keiser's withdrawal. The Turks, partly because of a language problem, pulled out prematurely, and Keiser's situation at Kunuri became critical. From 30 November to 1 December, the 2nd Division ran a bloody gauntlet from Kunuri south to Sunchon, losing a third of its strength and most of its artillery, vehicles, and equipment. The 1st Cavalry Division threw out a thin screen in front of the shattered column and Keiser took his division south of Pyongyang to Chungwha to re-form. By this time Walker had patched together a bow-shaped defensive line from Sukchon through Sunchon to Songchon.

The retreat of the 1st Marine Division began on 1 December. The 5th and 7th Marines, after bitter fighting, reached Hagaru on 3 December. On that day MacArthur reported to the JCS that X Corps was being withdrawn to Hungnam as rapidly as possible but that there was no 'practicability' in uniting it in a line with the Eighth Army – a line that would have to be 240km (150 miles) long and held

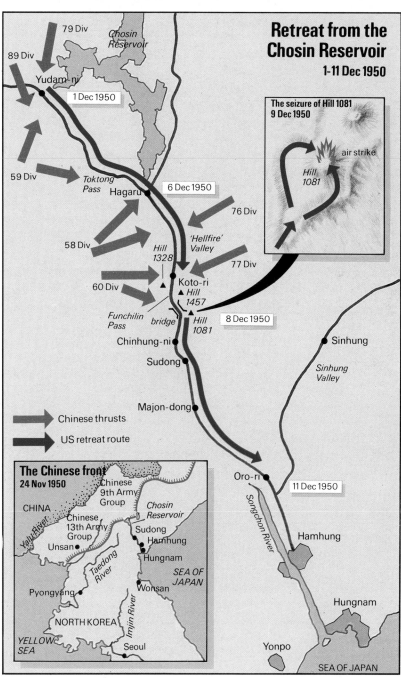

Below left: Marines take a break during the withdrawal from the Chosin Reservoir. The retreat was fraught with danger, especially during the crossing of the Funchilin Pass. Left: The fact that the long retreat went so smoothly was in large part due to the close air support that the Marines received. Right: Air services were always at full stretch in December 1950, and accidents were bound to occur. Here, the hulk of a C-46 lies on the airstrip at Wonju, having collided with other planes on landing.

alone by the seven American divisions, the combat effectiveness of the ROK army now being negligible. Without massive reinforcement, MacArthur saw no prospect except successive withdrawals to eventual beachhead 'bastions'.

Truman approved the reply drafted by the JCS: 'We consider that the preservation of your forces is now the primary consideration. Consolidation of forces into beachheads is concurred in.' Not having complete trust in MacArthur, Truman ordered the Army Chief of Staff, General Collins, to fly to Tokyo.

At a press conference on 30 November Truman had said that the United States would use every weapon it had, if neces-sary, to meet the military situation in Korea. This rattling of the nuclear sabre sent shivers through Europe and brought Britain's prime minister, Clement R. Attlee, to Washington on 4 December. He urged that an all-out war against China be avoided and that a ceasefire be sought. Already, the debates over the use of nuclear weapons and the 'limits' of this war were causing concern.

In Korea the withdrawal, or 'the big bug-out', as it was known by the troops, continued. Walker had drawn four fall-back lines on his map. The first line, 'Able', drawn north of Pyongyang, was overrun before it could be manned. Pyongyang itself was abandoned on 5 December, with 8000 to 10,000 tonnes of supplies left behind, broken up or burning. Evacuation of Pyongyang's port, Chinnampo, was completed the same day, Amphibious Group Three taking off 1800 American troops and 5800 ROK soldiers under air cover of Sea Furies and Fireflies from HMS *Theseus* and gunfire support from five British Commonwealth destroyers. Walker's next hope was the 'Baker' line, running along the Imjin River north of Seoul.

The air force commander, Lieutenant-General Stratemeyer, had promised that the FEAF would continue to maintain air superiority, furnish close support, and provide air transport, but a new factor had entered the air-power equation. On 1 November swept-wing MiG-15s, whose advanced design had originated in captured German data and which were spectacularly fast, had appeared over the Yalu River, out-classing the air force's F-80C Shooting Stars and the navy's F9F Pantherjets. First-line F-84E Thunderjets and F-86A Sabres were on their way to Korea but had not yet arrived.

Army Chief of Staff Collins arrived in Tokyo on 4 December, greeted Mac-Arthur, and continued on to Walker's HQ, which was now in Seoul. Walker told him that the Turkish Brigade and the US 2nd Division had been badly hurt but that the 1st Cavalry and the 24th and 25th Infantry Divisions were in good shape. He doubted if he could hold Seoul and a withdrawal from Inchon would be costly, but once united with X Corps he thought he would be able to hold the old Pusan Perimeter indefinitely. Collins spent the

5th visiting Milburn's I Corps command post and the 25th Division. He then went on to see Almond who met him on Yonpo airfield south of Hungnam. They visited the command posts of the US 3rd and 7th Infantry Divisions; Almond was confident that Hungnam could be held as long as was necessary. Collins spent most of the next day with MacArthur, whose chief point was that unless the UN Command was substantially reinforced it should be withdrawn. Collins said there might be four National Guard Divisions ready in April; MacArthur retorted that Chiang Kai-shek had 75,000 troops immediately available. Collins did not argue the point; his own estimate was that Walker and Almond could hold.

On 5 December, the same day that Pyongyang fell, General Tunner of the Combat Cargo Command flew into Hagaru with an offer to airlift out the encircled Marines if they would leave behind their vehicles and heavy equipment. Major-General Smith said no, the Marines would fight their way through. The break-out to Hungnam began the next day. The 100km (62-mile) march to the sea, covered magnificently by Marine and navy Vought F4U Corsairs and Douglas AD Skyraiders and including the fearsome descent through Funchilin Pass, was completed by the morning of 12 December. The Reservoir campaign had cost the Marines 4418 battle casualties, of whom 718 were dead, 192 missing, and 3508 wounded.

Fortunately for the air umbrella over the Eighth Army and X Corps, the much-feared MiG-15s stayed close to the Yalu. They had limited range and their Chinese pilots were inexperienced, particularly in gunnery. Continued UN air superiority was further assured by the arrival of the F-84E Thunderjets and F-86A Sabres. The F-84s flew their first mission from Taegu airfield on 6 December and the even more advanced F-86s took off from Kimpo on 17 December, immediately scoring their first kills. The F-86 Sabres, like the MiGs, had benefited in their swept-wing design from the innovative German aviation engineers.

Rear-Admiral Doyle, the expert on amphibious operations, took personal charge of the Hungnam evacuation,

directing operations from his flagship *Mount McKinley*. Wonsan was already evacuated. Transport Division Eleven had taken out 3834 troops, 7009 refugees, 1146 vehicles, and around 10,000 tonnes of cargo while the naval guns of the cruiser *St Paul* and destroyers *Sperry* and *Zellars* held the enemy at a respectable distance. At Hungnam, Almond's operation order called for the Marines and the remaining ROK troops to leave first, followed by the US 7th and 3rd Divisions. Almond was to reassemble his US divisions in the Pusan–Usan–Masan area in South Korea. The ROK I Corps, on arrival at Samchok, was to revert to ROK army control.

For naval gunfire coverage of the Hungnam evacuation there was the battleship *Missouri,* the cruisers *St Paul* and *Rochester,* seven destroyers, and four rocket ships. On 15 December, as the last of the Marines sailed for Pusan, the big ships began their deep naval gunfire support at ranges up to 16km (10 miles).

Rear-Admiral Ewen's Task Force 77 had grown to four fast carriers – *Philippine Sea, Leyte, Valley Forge,* and *Princeton* – plus the light carrier *Bataan* and the escort carriers *Badoeng Strait* and *Sicily*. The Corsairs and Skyraiders continued to work the snow-covered hills.

The last of the ROK troops left for Samchok on 18 December; the last of the US 7th Division was under way by 21 December. *Missouri* began 16-in main battery fire on 23 December. Naval gunfire went on around the clock and by the 24th had concentrated down to a box 2300m (2500yd) wide and 3200m (3500yd)

deep. All of Major-General Robert H. Soule's 3rd Division was off the beach by mid-afternoon, Christmas Eve, and, as the ships exchanged 'Merry Christmas' signals, the whole waterfront went up in a planned demolition that included 400 tonnes of frozen dynamite and five hundred 450kg (1000lb) bombs. The navy had taken off 105,000 US and ROK servicemen, 91,000 refugees, 17,500 vehicles, and 350,000 tonnes of cargo in 109 navy and merchant ships.

There was sad news from the other side of the peninsula. On 23 December Walker was driving north from Seoul to visit the British 27th Brigade on the 'Baker' line when his jeep collided with a South Korean weapons carrier. The stocky 61-year-old general, a machine-gun officer in World War I and commander of US XX Corps in World War II, was killed.

In Washington, Lieutenant-General Matthew B. Ridgway, the army's deputy chief of staff for operations, was interrupted at a holiday dinner by a phone call from his chief. General Collins told him of Walker's death and that he, Ridgway, was the new commanding general of the Eighth Army. Ridgway reached Tokyo on Christmas Day and met MacArthur at the Dai-Ichi building the following morning. MacArthur directed him to defend 'in the most advanced positions in which you can maintain yourself'. In parting, Ridgway asked a last question: 'If I find the situation to my liking, would you have any objections to my attacking?'

'The Eighth Army is yours, Matt,' answered MacArthur grandly. 'Do what you think best.'

5. Ridgway's Offensive

The new commander of the Eighth US Army in Korea (EUSAK), General Matthew Ridgway, had commanded the 82nd Airborne Division and later the XVIII Airborne Corps in World War II, his distinguished record including the fighting in Normandy, the Battle of the Bulge and the 1945 Rhine crossing. His critics have suggested that in temperament he was a less subtle version of Douglas MacArthur. Indeed, a degree of self-advertisement was evident in the grenade which dangled from his paratrooper's belt, but such minor foibles were not uncommon among senior American officers. Unlike MacArthur, however, Ridgway became too involved in the details of the task in hand to incur the outright hostility of his political masters.

Arriving in Korea on 26 December 1950, he was deeply depressed by the state in which he found his command after its long ordeal. 'I must say in all frankness that the spirit of the Eighth Army gave me deep concern. There was a definite air of gloomy foreboding, of uncertainty, a spirit of apprehension as to what the future held. A good many of the unchanging principles of war seemed to have been forgotten.'

It was fortunate that his arrival coincided with a pause in the Chinese offensive (due to the enemy having outrun their supplies), since this gave him time to take stock. The Eighth Army numbered 365,000 men and was amply supplied and equipped. The largest contingents of the UN force were supplied by the United States and the Republic of Korea (ROK) itself, but troops from many nations were present and this in itself was encouraging. The United Kingdom and the Commonwealth had two brigades in the line, which could be relied on completely; there was also a Turkish brigade whose men had shown themselves to be hard, vindictive fighters; there were infantry battalions and supporting arms from Belgium, France, Greece and the Philippines; and more national contingents of ground troops were on their way, including a reinforced Canadian brigade.

The crisis facing Ridgway, therefore, was one of morale, and this he set about

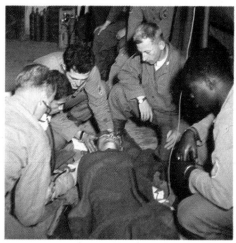

resolving in several ways. First, he insisted that commanders at all levels should exercise their function in the combat zone rather than in their rear command posts, and be seen by their men to be doing so. Secondly, aggressive patrolling was introduced along the front with the intention of restoring confidence by small tactical successes. Thirdly, he decided that holding ground was of less importance than stripping bare the enemy's principal asset, his vast manpower resources, and to this end devised the method of fighting known as 'the Meatgrinder', which took full advantage of the communists' dependence on infantry. Quite simply, this meant that every possible source of firepower, including aircraft, artillery and tanks, was to be devoted entirely to killing Chinese.

Ridgway barely had time to assess the situation and state his policy before the communists resumed their offensive on 1 January 1951. This found Milburn's I Corps (US 24th and 3rd Divisions, ROK 1st Division, the Turkish brigade and the

British 29th Brigade) holding the UN left, west of the Seoul corridor; Coulter's IX Corps (US 1st Cavalry and 25th Divisions, ROK 6th Division, the Commonwealth 27th Brigade, the Greek and Philippine battalions) in the centre; and the ROK I and III Corps on the right; the line running from a point north of Inchon on the west coast to Yangyang on the east. In immediate reserve was the 1st Marine Division and, further south, Almond's X Corps re-fitting around Pusan.

Bugles blowing and whistles shrilling, the Chinese swarmed forward in their usual *hachi-shiki* formation, a 'V' open towards the objective, which was quickly isolated by the arms of the formation, then surrounded and swamped. The ROK formations were particularly hard-hit and Ridgway watched uneasily as they fled, abandoning their equipment, packed tight aboard their trucks, their only thought to distance themselves as far as possible from the front. The following day the gaps in the front were plugged by

Opposite page: A 'Long Tom' blasts away at communist positions during a night bombardment. Extensive use of artillery was to be the hallmark of US tactics in Korea. Top: Matthew B. Ridgway (on left of photograph, here conferring with Brigadier-General Van Brunt) took over the US Eighth Army after General Walker's death. Ridgway's first task was to stabilise the situation in Korea. For by the New Year the UN troops had pulled back from Seoul (above left, UN forces cross one of the last pontoon bridges across the Han River just to the north of the city) and casualties were mounting (above, a badly wounded US soldier is treated in a forward field hospital).

the 1st Marine Division and by X Corps, hastening north to edge into the line between IX Corps and the main body of the ROK army. The majority of the UN troops had benefited from the pause in the Chinese offensive and the experience of the previous year. They now knew what to expect from a Chinese attack. It was a dangerous situation, but on this occasion the response was more controlled and measured than it had been when the Chinese Communist Forces (CCF) had launched their initial offensive the previous November. On the sector held by the British 29th Brigade (1st Battalion The Gloucestershire Regiment, 1st Battalion Royal Northumberland Fusiliers and 1st Battalion Royal Ulster Rifles) the enemy had by 3 January succeeded in isolating three of the Fusiliers' four rifle companies. They were in no immediate danger and were resisting strongly, but the fact remained that they would have to be extricated fairly quickly.

Flaming Crocodiles

The means to achieve this fortunately existed in the form of C Squadron, 7th Royal Tank Regiment, which had arrived in Korea the previous November equipped with the terrible Churchill Crocodiles. No opportunity had presented itself for using the flamethrowers with which these tanks were fitted, and at the start of the New Year offensive the squadron had

dropped all but one of its trailers and driven forward to fight as gun tanks. Despite its World War II vintage the Churchill was well-armoured and every bit as nimble as the Centurion on the difficult Korean terrain, an important consideration since the trapped companies could only be reached by a narrow, ice-covered track which passed through a difficult defile. Together with the Fusiliers' fourth company, C Squadron's 5 Troop and two HQ tanks mounted a counter-attack along this axis. It was very successful; two companies were relieved and the third was able to break out at last light. Infantry casualties suffered during the counter-attack were light owing to the high rate of fire put down by the tanks, but CCF casualties were estimated at around 150.

Despite such local successes much valuable ground was lost and as the battle developed it became clear that the enemy's objectives were Seoul and the railway centre of Wonju. Ridgway decided that neither could be held and, once more, the pitiful columns of refugees began streaming south from the capital with such of their possessions as they could carry. By the evening of 4 January the city was again under communist control. The offensive continued for a further three weeks but the UN line held, absorbing the weight of continuous attacks. In contrast to their spectacular gains of 1950, the Chinese only succeeded in pushing the

front some 55km (35 miles) south to the line Pyongtaek–Samchok, and then only at horrific cost. By 24 January they were incapable of further effort.

The principal reason for this was that Ridgway's Meatgrinder was becoming more and more efficient with every day that passed. Time after time the Chinese and North Korean human waves of advancing infantry were blown apart on artillery killing-grounds, raked by the fire of tanks and automatic weapons and strafed without pause from the air. Against such firepower the CCF and Korean People's Army (KPA), lacking air superiority or an effective tank arm, could deploy only their mortars and the few artillery weapons they had with them and could maintain in action. This revealed in the most glaringly obvious fashion the folly of committing lightly armed, mobile troops against fully equipped divisions in open country. As if this were not enough, the further the communists advanced the more acute their supply difficulties became. Much of their daily requirement travelled down the railway which skirted the east coast of North Korea, and this was subjected to constant interference and occasional demolition by Royal Marine Special Boat Squadron teams landing from US submarines. The remainder, in the absence of mechanical transport, had to be man-packed all the way to the front,

General Ridgway (opposite page top, talking to a wounded soldier) devised a set of tactics known as 'the Meatgrinder'. (He may have got this phrase from George Patton, the great World War II general. Patton used it in a graphic metaphor to his superior General Bradley, explaining how, during the campaign for northern Europe, the Germans had got their head stuck in the meatgrinder, and that he – Patton – had got hold of the handle.) In Korea, the Meatgrinder meant a steady war of attrition using artillery (left) and all the weight of US support weaponry – from flamethrowers (opposite page bottom) to rockets (below).

where the wretched porters became as vulnerable as the troops to the all-embracing Meatgrinder.

For their part, the UN troops now had the measure of the enemy and had recovered their self-confidence. Even the Americans' sense of humour was reviving. The wild press reports about Chinese 'hordes' led to speculation among the US troops as to the precise number of platoons needed to make up an average-sized Chinese horde!

The rundown of the offensive coincided with the departure from Korea of General Lin Piao, commander of the CCF in Korea and architect of its November victories. Some sources suggest that Lin was wounded, others that the strain of watching his army fight itself to destruction had exhausted him. His replacement was General Peng Teh-huai, a former Nationalist officer who had served in Tibet and who was as noted for his coarse ways and harsh tongue as he was for his streak of obstinacy. While Peng commanded the CCF from GHQ in Mukden, Kim Il Sung was technically the supreme

commander of the joint KPA/CCF HQ near Pyongyang – however it was Peng who was really in charge because of his direct control of massive Chinese forces. It was Peng's misfortune that he should inherit a battle which had already gone sour.

The enemy's exhaustion was confirmed during a sortie made by the 27th Regimental Combat Team ('the Wolfhounds') which revealed that the communists were merely consolidating their gains. Ridgway decided to put them under immediate pressure and on 25 January commenced a general advance to the Han River under the operational codename of 'Thunderbolt'. Despite its title, Thunderbolt was an intentionally slow-moving, attritional operation designed to capture successive enemy positions not by storming them but by killing their occupants where they stood. The Chinese, fighting desperately to preserve the gains won at such terrible cost, died in their foxholes under concentrated artillery fire or were incinerated by repeated napalm strikes. By 9 February

the enemy's resistance had all but collapsed; Inchon fell without a struggle, as did the strategically important Kimpo airfield, and Wonju was recaptured. Sensing that he was now confronted by mere remnants of the communist forces, Ridgway maintained the pressure in a follow-through operation named 'Roundup'.

Such optimism was slightly premature. Logic indeed dictated that Peng should break contact and withdraw the survivors of his army closer to their supply bases, but a question of face was involved and his stubborn nature refused to accept defeat. He had asked for, and been granted, massive reinforcement, and on 11 February the first three divisions to arrive were thrown into a spoiling attack directed against X Corps in the centre of the line.

The object of the attack was to recapture an important road junction at Chip-

yong-ni, the loss of which would seriously disrupt further UN progress to the north. Holding Chipyong-ni was an outstandingly efficient US unit, the 23rd Infantry Regiment under Colonel Paul Freeman, with an equally good French battalion under command. Freeman established a strong perimeter with his 1st battalion covering the northern face, his 3rd the eastern, his 2nd the southern and the French the western. Completely surrounded, his command fought off suicidal 'human-wave' attacks which surged forward to envelop the defences, often ending in fierce hand-to-hand combat, the garrison being supported the while by X Corps artillery and air strikes. The French battalion commanded by Lieutenant-Colonel Raoul Montclar, a tough individual who had served in the Foreign Legion under a *nom de guerre*, particularly distinguished itself. Somewhere, the battalion had acquired a hand-wound siren,

the dismal wails of which echoed around the valley and completely eclipsed the comparatively puny efforts of the communist buglers. On the first occasion it was used the Chinese assault wave came to a complete halt, nonplussed; Montclar's men went for them with the bayonet, and traditional French *élan* swept them off the field.

Hammer and anvil

On 14 February Freeman's prodigious ammunition expenditure was made good by a parachute supply drop, while elsewhere X Corps brought the enemy's spoiling attack under control. The following day a task force from the 5th Cavalry Regiment set out to relieve Chipyong-ni under the command of Colonel Marcel

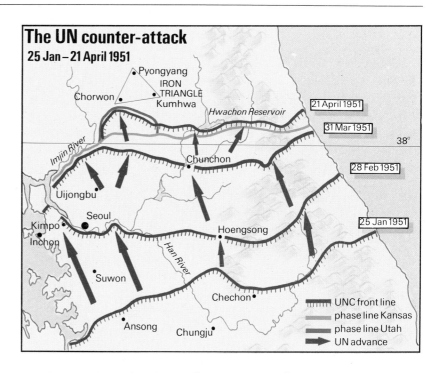

The UN counter-attack
25 Jan – 21 April 1951

- 21 April 1951
- 31 Mar 1951
- 28 Feb 1951
- 25 Jan 1951

38°

Pyongyang
IRON
TRIANGLE
Chorwon
Kumhwa
Hwachon Reservoir
Chunchon
Imjin River
Uijongbu
Seoul
Kimpo
Hoengsong
Inchon
Han River
Suwon
Chechon
Ansong
Chungju

⊤⊤⊤⊤⊤ UNC front line
—— phase line Kansas
—— phase line Utah
➤ UN advance

Opposite page: The crew of a US 8-in howitzer lay down a barrage, acting on instructions from a forward observation officer. Good fire control was the key to the effectiveness of UN artillery. Left: Sergeant Mike Chalooga of the 5th Regimental Combat Team poses by the body of a dead KPA soldier, near the Han River in February 1951.

Crambez. Stiff opposition was encountered and since speed was essential Crambez decided to make the last 11km (7 miles) of his run with his 23 tanks and as much infantry as they could carry on their engine decks. The latter suffered cruelly as the route lay along a valley lined with mortar and machine-gun positions. On the other hand, their presence was essential to protect the tanks against close-quarter attack; even so, two tanks were destroyed by the enemy's bazooka teams. Crambez broke through into the rear of a regiment which was forming up for an attack on the 23rd Infantry's perimeter. Panic-stricken, the Chinese bolted towards Freeman's lines, being caught between the hammer and the anvil, with predictable results.

Following the relief of Chipyong-ni, Peng bowed to the inevitable. By the 19th the initiative had unmistakably returned to the Eighth Army and on the 21st Ridgway mounted Operation Killer with IX and X Corps, designed to trap and destroy as many of the enemy as possible before they could re-cross the Han. Aware of the effect that sustained carnage was having on Chinese morale, he had leaflets dropped on the retreating columns; they read, simply: COUNT YOUR MEN. However, lacking heavy equipment, the communists were able to disengage rapidly and withdraw out of immediate danger.

Killer was followed on 7 March by Operation Ripper. This required the

ROK army to fight holding actions at the eastern end of the line while I Corps stood fast on the Han and IX and X Corps fought their way across the river. The success of this operation placed Seoul inside an untenable salient, forcing Peng to abandon it on the 15th. At this point I Corps joined the offensive, dropping the 187th Airborne Regiment on Munsan-ni, 30km (19 miles) northwest of Seoul, and then pushing out an armoured task force to join it. This operation trapped fewer of the enemy than had been expected, and this in itself was some indication of the pace at which Peng's divisions were now withdrawing. However, it provided I

Corps with a footing on the Imjin River.

Thus far MacArthur had let his subordinate fight the battle in his own way, but now he sounded a note of caution. 'As our battle lines shift north the supply position of the enemy will progressively improve, just as inversely the effectiveness of our air potential will progressively diminish, this in turn causing his numerical ground superiority to become of increasing battlefield significance.' The consequences of this, he added with considerable prescience, would be that 'the battle lines cannot fail in time to reach a point of theoretical stalemate'. Ridgway's rejoinder that 'We didn't set out to conquer

China – we set out to stop communism,' was needlessly tart, but was clearly intended to convey that he did not intend repeating the errors of judgement made by the commander-in-chief the previous year.

Into the Iron Triangle

Nevertheless, MacArthur's comments were obviously valid. The further Peng retired, the more his situation eased. Moreover, since neither Stalin nor Mao Tse-tung was prepared to accept so obvious a defeat, new Russian equipment and fresh Chinese divisions were already streaming into Korea. Rallying behind his exhausted rearguards in an area known as the Iron Triangle, Peng immediately began preparing a counter-offensive intended to bring about a conclusive communist victory. He had learned much from his mauling by Ridgway, particularly regarding the value of artillery, and although he could never hope to match the United Nations in this sphere, he could at least ensure that in future his major attacks received a reasonable degree of support.

Meanwhile, MacArthur was dismissed on 11 April (see following chapter). His place was taken by Ridgway, who handed over command of the Eighth Army to General James Van Fleet. The task facing Van Fleet was not ostensibly onerous, for there was already agreement between the allies that their war aims did not extend to the reunification of the Korean peninsula by force. His troops were now operating north of the 38th parallel and, although very tired after four months of more or less continuous action, were still advancing. It remained only to secure a line which was defensible to complete the task begun in January.

By 14 April, as a result of Operation Rugged, all UN troops were in position along such a line and the process of digging, wiring and general consolidation began. This had not been completed when, on 17 April, the Chinese began probing the defences with unexpected aggression. These local clashes, while fierce, were merely the first rumblings of the storm which would break over the Eighth Army four days later.

The UN offensive of January-February 1951 forced the communist armies back north of Seoul. Opposite page bottom: An American sentry looks out over the frozen Han River while smoke rises from an air strike on Seoul itself, carried out by Royal Navy Corsair aircraft. Opposite page top: Some of the Chinese communist prisoners taken during this period of the war. Below: By the early months of 1951, the UN forces were far better prepared to face the extremes of the Korean winter, and their clothing reflected a new awareness of the basics necessary for infantrymen to function properly.

6. The United Nations Command

Due to the 14-hour time difference, the telegram from the US ambassador in Seoul, John Muccio, conveying the first official news of the North Korean invasion of the South, arrived in Washington DC on the evening of Saturday 24 June 1950. The Assistant Secretary of State for Far Eastern Affairs, Dean Rusk, was summoned from a party and he telephoned Secretary of State Dean Acheson. In turn, Acheson telephoned President Truman at his weekend Missouri home and suggested convening the UN Security Council. Around midnight the Assistant Secretary of State for UN Affairs, John D. Hickerson, telephoned UN Secretary General Trygve Lie. According to Hickerson, Lie responded to the news with: 'My God, Jack, that's against the charter of the United Nations.'

When the Security Council met at 2.20pm on 25 June it was still not entirely clear whether the North or the South had initiated the fighting. Several hours elapsed before a resolution was passed by nine votes (those of Nationalist China, Cuba, Egypt, Ecuador, France, India, Norway, the United Kingdom, and the United States) to nil, with one abstention (Yugoslavia) which noted 'with grave concern the armed invasion of the Republic of Korea by armed forces from North Korea', determined this a 'breach of the peace' and called upon the North to cease hostilities and withdraw.

The Soviet Union failed to exercise a veto because it had boycotted the Security Council since January 1950 in protest at the Nationalist Chinese continuing to occupy the Chinese seat on the Council despite their eviction from the mainland

by the communists. The Soviets also missed the opportunity to veto the subsequent resolution of 27 June by which members of the United Nations were requested to assist South Korea. They subsequently claimed that the Korean conflict was an internal one and that the UN decisions were illegal since they were taken in the absence of both themselves and the Chinese communists. By contrast the United States claimed that the United Nations was morally committed to South Korea, even though it was not a UN member, since the UN had effectively created the state by the supervised elections of 1948. The British prime minister, Clement Attlee, also remarked in the House of Commons on 5 July that Article 51 of the UN Charter authorised all states to defend themselves, whether members or not, and that any other state was entitled to defend one subjected to aggression since such aggression endangered all. Even had the Soviets exercised the veto, the United States could still have gone to

the General Assembly for approval. Indeed, the subsequent 'Uniting for Peace' resolution of the Assembly on 3 November 1950 provided for such a contingency in the future.

Security Council resolution

Irrespective of the UN decisions, Truman had already moved to commit US forces to Korea. On the evening of 26 June the US Commander-in-Chief, Far East, General Douglas MacArthur, had been authorised to use air and naval forces to cover the evacuation of US citizens from the South. The US Seventh Fleet had also been ordered north to patrol the Straits of Formosa, thus preventing the Nationalists from escalating the conflict by invading the Chinese mainland. The resolution carried in the Security Council on the following afternoon by seven votes (Nationalist China, Cuba, Ecuador, France, Norway, the United Kingdom, and the United States) to one (Yugo-

out of 59 offered assistance. Of these, 15 including the United States provided troops, and five provided medical units.

In terms of ground forces, infantry battalions were provided by Australia (two), Belgium, Colombia, Ethiopia, France, Greece, the Netherlands, the Philippines and Thailand and infantry brigades by Canada, Turkey and the United Kingdom (two). Ground support units were supplied by Canada, New Zealand and the United Kingdom while Luxembourg provided a platoon in the Belgian battalion. Air squadrons were provided by Australia, Canada, Greece, South Africa and Thailand, and a total of 22 major naval vessels was provided by Australia, Canada, Colombia, France, the Netherlands, New Zealand, Thailand and the United Kingdom. In all, the contribution of UN members other than the United States amounted to around 40,000 ground personnel, over 30,000 naval personnel and 1100 air force personnel. The medical teams, totalling 2168 personnel, comprised a Danish Red Cross hospital ship, an Indian Field Ambulance Unit, an Italian Red Cross hospital, a Norwegian hospital unit and a Swedish Red Cross field hospital. By far the greatest contribution by a member of the UN was, of course, that of the United States, which at the end of the war had committed 302,483 ground troops out of a grand total of 932,539 ground forces under the UN Command in Korea. Other UN ground forces on 31 July 1953 totalled 39,145 men. The balance was made up by the Republic of Korea (ROK) forces. Many hundreds of thousands of

slavia) with two abstentions (Egypt and India) was taken as retrospective authorisation. In view of the North's failure to withdraw, the resolution requested that members 'furnish such assistance to the Republic of Korea as may be necessary to repel the armed attack and to restore international peace and security in the area'. As the situation deteriorated, MacArthur was authorised in the early hours of 30 June to commit US ground forces.

Other UN members had also begun to respond to the resolution. Australia, New Zealand and the United Kingdom had all placed naval forces at the disposal of the UN by 30 June. On 7 July the Security Council passed a further resolution by seven votes to three recommending that any forces offered be placed under a unified command. The United States was requested to nominate a commander, the United Nations Command formally coming into existence on 24 July. On 14 July Trygve Lie formally requested members to provide military assistance. Including the United States, some 42 member states

Above left: Douglas MacArthur meets Colonel Katzin, the personal representative of the UN secretary general. Far left: Commonwealth involvement in Korea. Canadian and British troops share a NAAFI. Left: A sign across a street in Korea welcomes the UN forces.

US naval and air personnel were also rotated through the US Far Eastern Command to fight in Korea, often while based in Japan. Not surprisingly, the 142,091 US casualties were far higher than the 17,260 casualties suffered by other UN members.

The Commonwealth Division

With the exception of ground forces from the British Commonwealth (Australia, Canada, New Zealand and the United Kingdom), which were constituted as the 1st Commonwealth Division in July 1951, the forces of other UN members were incorporated into US formations. The unified command also embraced the ROK army, which was placed under MacArthur's command by President Rhee on 14 July 1950, although it was never formally part of the US Eighth Army.

Initially the ROK army was a dubious addition. When US forces had withdrawn from South Korea in September 1948 they had left sufficient weapons for 50,000 men, but much of this equipment was obsolete. Moreover, the Americans had

envisaged the South Korean army as primarily a constabulary force with a limited defensive role. By June 1950 it numbered some 98,000 men but of these fewer than 68,000 were combat troops and only four of the eight divisions were anywhere near full strength. Most units had completed company training but few had started battalion training. The South Koreans had no tanks, no heavy artillery and only 27 armoured cars, while their 90-odd 105mm howitzers had a range of only 6600m (7200yd) compared to the 11,500m (12,500yd) range of the latest US version. The air force possessed only

The British Commonwealth made a valuable contribution to the UN effort. Left: Australian troops brew up some tea. Below: Canadian infantry in the field. Right: South African P-51 Mustangs after a raid on North Korea. Right below: Unloading supplies in Japan from a Canadair North Star aircraft.

22 trainer aircraft, ten of which they had had to purchase themselves from Canada. With so much antiquated equipment there were inevitable maintenance problems and in June 1950 over one-third of the army's vehicles were under repair, together with 15% of all weapons. Spare parts were all but exhausted and there were combat supplies for only six days. The situation was made worse by a reshuffle of major commands only 15 days before the invasion began and by the release, after the end of a period of alert, of large numbers of troops on furlough to assist with the harvest. When the North

Contributors to the UN Command	
Australia	Two infantry battalions, naval forces, one fighter squadron
Belgium	One infantry battalion
Canada	One reinforced infantry brigade, naval forces, one squadron of transport aircraft
Colombia	One infantry battalion, one naval frigate
Ethiopia	One infantry battalion
France	One reinforced infantry battalion
Great Britain	Two infantry brigades, one armoured regiment, one and a half artillery regiments, one and a half combat engineer regiments with supporting ground forces, the Far Eastern Fleet, two squadrons of Sunderlands
Greece	One infantry battalion, transport aircraft
Holland	One infantry battalion, naval forces
Luxembourg	One infantry company
New Zealand	One artillery regiment
Philippines	One infantry battalion, one company of tanks
South Africa	One fighter squadron
Thailand	One infantry battalion, naval forces, air and naval transports
Turkey	One infantry brigade
medical aid	Denmark, India, Italy, Norway, Sweden

Korean invasion began, only a third of the South Korean troops were actually in the front line, defence plans did not exist below divisional level and by 4 August the army had been reduced to barely 45,000 men.

One requirement for the UN Command was therefore to rebuild the confidence and strength of the ROK army. In August 1950 several thousand South Korean recruits were inducted directly into the US Army under the 'Katusa' scheme (Korean Augmentation to US Army) to compensate for American casualties and to be properly trained. The scheme foundered on communication difficulties and was dropped by the end of the year. It was only after the front had been stabilised in the summer of 1951 that it was possible to begin retraining the ROK army in earnest, priority being given to the development of leadership and to remedying deficiencies in artillery support. There was some subsequent discussion among the US Joint Chiefs of Staff (JCS) on the appropriate size for the new army. General James Van Fleet, who had taken command of the Eighth Army in April 1951, favoured expansion beyond the ten-division, 250,000-strong force envisaged by the JCS, while his predecessor (now promoted to UN Commander-in-Chief), General Matthew Ridgway, doubted their fighting ability, although he had been instrumental in pushing for their rearmament with 105mm and 155mm howitzers. The ROK army was in any case expanding rapidly and, when he succeeded Ridgway as UN Commander-in-Chief in May 1952, General Mark Clark also pressed for expansion. In April 1953 the JCS settled on 16 divisions,

and by the end of the war the South Koreans had over 600,000 men under arms. They had also suffered some 300,000 casualties during the course of the war.

When the overall command of UN forces was vested by the Security Council in an American nominee in July 1950, this had naturally meant MacArthur. As Supreme Allied Commander in the Pacific during World War II, the flamboyant MacArthur had frequently clashed with his political and military superiors and as *de facto* ruler of Japan after its surrender in 1945 he had enjoyed considerable independence. He was also closely connected with the Republican Party, his name having been put forward unsuccessfully as a presidential candidate in 1948. Already bitterly critical of Truman's policy towards the Far East, MacArthur was suspicious of what he detected in the Administration as an excessive concern for Europe. Above all, he differed from Truman in his concept of how wars should be fought. While Truman and his UN partners were concerned to limit the

Above: The relative contributions of the nations that provided forces for the United Nations Command in Korea. The USA, of course, provided help that dwarfed that of any of the other nations.

extent of conflict and to prevent the intervention of either the communist Chinese or the Soviet Union, MacArthur's attitude could be summed up in his own famous pronouncement: 'There is no substitute for victory.'

The political divisions became apparent almost at once, when Chiang Kai-shek offered Nationalist troops to the Americans on 29 July 1950. MacArthur flew to meet Chiang at Truman's direction to explain why the offer would not be taken up, but the tone of Chiang's communiqué after the meeting and MacArthur's praise of the Nationalists rang alarm bells in Washington. Averell Harriman was dispatched to spell out official policy on Formosa to MacArthur. On 17 August, however, MacArthur in responding to an invitation to send a message to the Veterans of Foreign Wars, an American ex-serviceman's organisation about to hold its annual convention, chose to deliver a thinly veiled attack on official

attitudes towards Nationalist participation. The text was released to the press on 26 August despite efforts in Washington to suppress it.

Purely military disputes had also arisen, the JCS being worried by MacArthur's ambitious plan for the Inchon landings. There was then the issue of how far northwards the subsequent UN advance should proceed. On 27 September the JCS authorised MacArthur to cross the 38th parallel but directed him to submit all operational plans in advance and neither to cross the frontier between North Korea and China – the Yalu River – nor to violate Chinese airspace. The advance was approved by the UN General Assembly on 7 October, the UN thus committing itself to the unification of the Korean peninsula by force of arms.

Debate on Wake

Truman then decided to go to meet MacArthur, possibly as an attempt to gain political kudos for the forthcoming congressional elections, but also to spell out Administration policy. In the somewhat random discussion between the two men on Wake Island on 15 October neither fully comprehended the views of the other, although Truman appears to have believed that he had imposed some degree of understanding on MacArthur. The most significant part of the discussion was MacArthur's confident assertion that the Chinese would not intervene as the UN forces neared the Yalu. Secure in this belief, MacArthur was soon lifting operational restrictions imposed by the JCS in September, to which the JCS made no response. The point of departure came, however, on 5 November when the JCS discovered that MacArthur had ordered the bombing of the Yalu bridges. The JCS refused to allow the planned B-29 Superfortress air strike although they did subsequently authorise MacArthur to bomb the half of the bridges that lay in North Korean territory. MacArthur then requested permission to pursue North Korean aircraft into Chinese airspace but this was also refused.

By this time the extent of Chinese intervention was becoming apparent, and the UN forces were suffering from

MacArthur's failure to believe his intelligence sources and also from his earlier decision to keep the Eighth Army separated from X Corps. On 28 November, as the Chinese offensive intensified, MacArthur requested permission to bomb Manchurian airfields, and demanded that the Chinese Nationalists be unleashed against the mainland. Asked for his comments on a JCS plan to evacuate the Korean peninsula altogether, MacArthur submitted four proposals on 30 December: that China be economically blockaded; that China be blockaded by sea; that Chinese airfields and industrial targets be bombed; and that the Nationalists

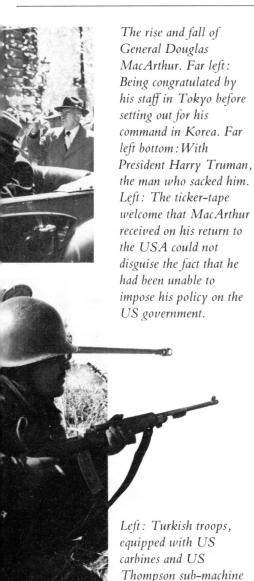

The rise and fall of General Douglas MacArthur. Far left: Being congratulated by his staff in Tokyo before setting out for his command in Korea. Far left bottom: With President Harry Truman, the man who sacked him. Left: The ticker-tape welcome that MacArthur received on his return to the USA could not disguise the fact that he had been unable to impose his policy on the US government.

Left: Turkish troops, equipped with US carbines and US Thompson sub-machine guns. Below right: MacArthur with the man who succeeded him, Matthew Ridgway.

launch a diversion by invading China. All his proposals were rejected by the JCS on 9 January 1951 despite MacArthur claiming that the position in Korea would be untenable unless his plan was adopted. He later erroneously claimed that the JCS had endorsed his ideas in a paper of 12 January when, in fact, they had merely considered them among other options in the event of the UN forces being forced off the peninsula. On 14 January MacArthur again requested permission to attack the communists' 'privileged sanctuary', now claiming that it would prevent stalemate – since Ridgway was rapidly stabilising a situation MacArthur

had claimed was hopeless. On 11 February he not only suggested bombing the Yalu bridges but cutting off Manchuria with a cordon of radioactive waste. The JCS again rejected his ideas.

Provoking the President

MacArthur's actions now became increasingly provocative to Truman. On 20 March 1951 he was made aware of JCS proposals for seeking a ceasefire and deliberately sabotaged the initiative by issuing an insulting public ultimatum to the Chinese on 24 March which they were bound to reject. Truman had thought of dismissing MacArthur as early as August 1950 but the political climate had not seemed opportune. On 5 April, however, the Republican leader in the House of Representatives, Joe Martin, read out a letter written to him by MacArthur on 24 March denigrating the concentration on European affairs and urging the use of the Nationalists. This directly contravened a presidential instruction of 6 December that theatre commanders should not make foreign policy statements without clearance. Recently released declassified documents have also revealed that the National Security Agency had intercepted cables from Spanish and Portuguese diplomats to their home governments in the last week of March in which they reported private conversations with MacArthur. In these conversations MacArthur had made it clear that he intended to continue to defy Truman and that he favoured the use of nuclear weapons against the Chinese even at the risk of war with the Soviet

Union. In a series of meetings between 6 and 9 April 1951 Truman and the JCS took the decision that MacArthur must be dismissed and that political control over an over-mighty military subject must be fully re-asserted. Unfortunately, due to a press leak, MacArthur learned of his dismissal at second hand – a sad end to a great career.

Considerable controversy surrounded the dismissal in the United States. Over 78,000 telegrams were received at the White House supporting MacArthur by a ratio of over 20:1, while a gallup poll showed that Truman was supported by only 29% of those asked. MacArthur, who had surrendered his command to Ridgway, returned to an enthusiastic welcome in San Francisco on 17 April and addressed Congress on 19 April. He was also accorded a massive and enthusiastic ticker-tape reception in New York. However, the bubble of his popularity was to be burst by the subsequent series of hearings by the Joint Senate Foreign Relations and Armed Services committees between 3 May and 25 June 1951, in which MacArthur's claims were minutely dissected and exposed as highly dangerous. As the chairman of the JCS, Omar Bradley, memorably expressed it, Korea was 'the wrong war, at the wrong place, at the wrong time, and with the wrong enemy . . .'. MacArthur had a kind of victory in reinforcing Truman's decision not to stand for re-election, but it was the Administration's concept of limiting the war and maintaining strict control of the military that ultimately triumphed over the opinions of the great general.

7. The Chinese Counterattack

General James Van Fleet, new commander of the United Nations troops in Korea, was a product of the famous West Point Class of 1915, which had also included Generals Dwight D. Eisenhower and Omar Bradley. He had served in Europe during World War II, commanding first a division and then a corps, and subsequently acted as US adviser to the victorious anti-communist forces during the Greek civil war. His methods were very similar to Ridgway's, his basic philosophy being that 'we must expend steel and fire, not men,' and he placed even greater emphasis on the artillery's participation. 'I want so many artillery holes

that a man can step from one to the other,' he had commented shortly after assuming command, and in consequence the artillery shell consumption soon reached five times its normal level. The extra physical burden placed on the logistic services and on the sweating gunners themselves was collectively termed the 'Van Fleet Load', and the expense involved caused grumbling among congressmen for years afterwards, but it produced the required results.

As April wore on clear evidence became available regarding the huge Chinese build-up within the Iron Triangle and elsewhere in North Korea. That Peng was about to return to the attack was

beyond the slightest doubt, and Van Fleet was determined, as he put it, to 'roll with the punch', yet still retain as much as possible of the ground won during Ridgway's recent counter-offensive.

He would have been greatly encouraged had he been aware of the concern with which the Chinese themselves were now viewing the war. Even China had limits to her reserves of trained manpower, and, shaken by the slaughter of recent months, Mao had commented that 'a contest of attrition is unsuited to the Chinese Red Army'. Most of those who had swarmed over the Yalu River the previous year were now dead and their place had been

taken by men who had received only a few weeks' – or even days' – training before being marched south into Korea. The 1st Chinese Communist Forces (CCF) Field Army, as the Chinese People's Volunteers had now become, was therefore of mixed quality, and although it was better provided with artillery, Peng was deeply worried by the shortage of trained, experienced troops. In the event he was forced to resort to the cruel expedient of using his untrained formations to absorb the weight of the UN fire and swamp their defences, and then follow-through with his best units.

Peng had approximately 700,000 men under his command, of which half were to be committed during the first phase of the offensive. These were organised in three armies, which were really over-inflated, unwieldy corps. Much depended on the outcome of the offensive. If it succeeded, communist prestige would be restored and the campaign would continue; if it failed or ended in a bloody stalemate the whole Korean adventure would have to be ended by face-saving negotiation.

The offensive began on the crisp, moonlit night of 21/22 April and was directed at Van Fleet's I and IX Corps on the left of the line. On the IX Corps sector the Republic of Korea (ROK) 6th Division gave way, creating a gap between the 1st Marine and 24th Divisions. Both these formations offered a refused flank to the enemy and, obeying Van Fleet's instructions to roll with the punch, conducted an orderly withdrawal to the Hongchon River, where the line was again stabilised on 24 April.

It was, however, against I Corps that Peng directed his principal thrust. This was to be made by the 63rd Army, composed of the 187th, 188th and 189th Divisions, each about 9000 strong and containing a high percentage of the most experienced and battle-hardened troops available. The plan involved a rapid march to the Imjin River commencing on 21 April, the breaking of the Allied front there, and an immediate advance on

Seoul down the traditional invasion route, the effect being to isolate a major part of I Corps, which would be trapped with its back to the sea. Peng had stressed that speed was essential and he expected his leading elements to reach Seoul within 36 hours of crossing their start-lines. These plans were to founder on the jagged rock of the British 29th Brigade, which lay directly across the path of the 63rd Army.

The 29th Brigade, commanded by Brigadier Tom Brodie, consisted of the 1st Battalions each of the Royal Northumberland Fusiliers (Lieutenant-Colonel Kingsley-Foster), the Gloucestershire Regiment (Lieutenant-Colonel J. P. Carne) and the Royal Ulster Rifles (Lieutenant-Colonel Carson), plus a small Belgian battalion commanded by Lieutenant-Colonel B. E. M. Crahay. In immediate support were the 25-pounders

The renewed offensive by the communist forces in April 1951 led to some of the heaviest fighting of the war. Above and left: US troops go into action, under cover of the artillery barrages that the new commander of UN ground forces, James Van Fleet, had decided were the key to success. Far left: One of the artillery pieces that pounded the communists to such devastating effect: an 8-in howitzer mounted on a Sherman chassis.

of 45 Field Regiment, Royal Artillery (RA), and the 4.2-in mortars of 170 Mortar Battery, RA, one troop of the latter being attached to each of the brigade's battalions; and some kilometres to the rear were the Centurion tanks of the 8th King's Royal Irish Hussars.

The tremendous achievements of this remarkable brigade become more intelligible if it is remembered that regimental *esprit de corps* and tradition play a most significant role in British military life. Because of this, each regiment is quite convinced that it is better at its job than others in the same branch of service and will point to incidents in its long history to emphasise the point. The three infantry battalions were drawn from that long line of county regiments which had served throughout the British Empire for two and a half centuries, and had won their battle honours on every one of the world's continents. They had been expanded ten- and twenty-fold during the World Wars and their ranks in Korea were filled by young National Servicemen (conscripts) and regular soldiers of various ages. The largest group, however, consisted of recalled regular reservists, most of whom had seen active service in World War II and were already veterans.

Brigadier Brodie was responsible for a 15km (9-mile) sector of the front. On the right he deployed the Belgian battalion on a high feature beyond the river, its flank and rear protected by the confluence of the Hantan with the Imjin, and beyond this point the UN line swung away to the

north. The centre of the brigade's position was held by the Fusiliers and the left by the Glosters, with the Royal Ulster Rifles, for the moment, in brigade reserve some 3km (2 miles) behind the front. On the Glosters' left was the ROK 1st Division, which held the line westwards to the sea. The entire position was dominated by a high feature known as Kamak-San, from which it was possible to look down on the area occupied by the forward battalions. Two defiles carried tracks from the Imjin to the south through this range, the one passing through the Fusiliers' position being comparatively minor; the one controlled by the Glosters, however, was better in every way and its capture was a vital element in Peng's strategy. To the front, the protection offered by the Imjin

Top: North-bound UN transport fords the Imjin River before the communist offensive of April 1951. Above: The original assault on 'Hill 327' that secured the position for UN forces in February. Right: A British heavy machine gun post just north of the Imjin River. The weapon is a water-cooled model, such as had been the mainstay of infantry units in defensive positions since World War I.

was welcome but of limited value, for although the river was 275m (300yd) wide it was fordable in many places. Much of the terrain, while barren in the agricultural sense, was covered in low scrub which favoured the enemy's tactics of infiltration. In general, the brigade's deployment made the best possible use of the resources available, although battalion commanders had rather less wire, mines and trip flares than they would have wished. In the final analysis, it seems unlikely that such shortages influenced events to any great extent.

Castle Hill

Whatever happened elsewhere on the brigade's sector, it was reasonably certain that the Glosters would be hit hard. On 22 April the battalion was deployed as follows: A Company (Major P. A. Angier) was on Point 148, better known as Castle Hill because of a concrete observation bunker erected on the forward slope by US Army engineers, above the hamlet of Choksong and covering the main Imjin ford; D Company (Captain M. G. Harvey) was on Point 182, some 1400m (1530yd) to the southeast; B Company (Major E. D. Harding) lay some way to the east of this on Point 144, and beyond them was a 3km (2-mile) gap separating the Glosters from the Fusiliers; C Company (Major P. B. Mitchell) lay in reserve on a narrow ridge overlooking the defile in which Battalion HQ, the 3-in mortar platoon and the 4.2-in mortars of C Troop, 170 Battery, were located, a little to the north of the village of Solma-ri; across the defile and on Point 235 was the assault pioneer platoon; and dispersed where it would do most good was the battalion's Vickers medium machine-gun platoon. Excluding the battalion's A, B and F transport echelons and the 'Left Out of Battle Party', there were a total of 657 Glosters in the line, 46 members of C Troop, the 32-strong Observation Post parties of 70 Field Battery (45 Regiment, RA), and 38 attached personnel from other arms, including armourers, cooks and signallers: a grand total of 773 men.

Mere dispositions and numbers, however, tell only part of the story, for two other factors were simultaneously at work. At the battle of Alexandria in 1801 the Glosters were engaged in a furious firefight with a French regiment to their front when they were simultaneously attacked from behind. The rear rank had promptly faced about and dealt with the situation, and in recognition of the event the regiment was granted the right to wear a duplicate of its badge on the rear of its headdress. Every Gloster since had been taught to take pride in the story and, if necessary, they were quite prepared to fight 'Back to Back' again. Now, the strength of the old tradition was to be tested anew, in an inferno such as the men of Alexandria could never have imagined.

The second factor was Lieutenant-Colonel James Carne, the battalion's commanding officer. A quiet man who solved his problems with the aid of a contemplative pipe, Carne was a first-rate infantryman who had already been awarded the Distinguished Service Order (DSO) for an earlier action in the campaign. He was deeply hurt by casualties among his men, and although he tried hard to conceal the fact the signs were visible to those who knew him well. Most important of all, James Carne was a natural and inspiring leader of men.

The first contact with the enemy came at 2200 hours on the night of 21 April, when a three-man listening post down at the ford – which was known as Gloster Crossing – detected a 14-strong Chinese

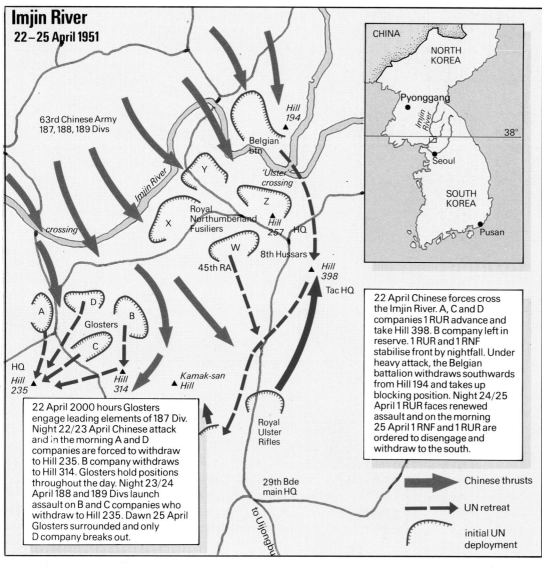

Imjin River
22–25 April 1951

63rd Chinese Army
187, 188, 189 Divs

Hill 194

Belgian btn

Imjin River

'Ulster crossing

Y

Z

Royal Northumberland Fusiliers

X

Hill 257

HQ

crossing

W

8th Hussars

45th RA

Hill 398

Tac HQ

A

D

B

Glosters

C

HQ
Hill 235

Hill 314

Kamak-san Hill

Royal Ulster Rifles

29th Bde main HQ

to Uijongbu

CHINA

NORTH KOREA

Pyonggang

Imjin River

38°

Seoul

SOUTH KOREA

Pusan

22 April Chinese forces cross the Imjin River. A, C and D companies 1 RUR advance and take Hill 398. B company left in reserve. 1 RUR and 1 RNF stabilise front by nightfall. Under heavy attack, the Belgian battalion withdraws southwards from Hill 194 and takes up blocking position. Night 24/25 April 1 RUR faces renewed assault and on the morning 25 April 1 RNF and 1 RUR are ordered to disengage and withdraw to the south.

22 April 2000 hours Glosters engage leading elements of 187 Div. Night 22/23 April Chinese attack and in the morning A and D companies are forced to withdraw to Hill 235. B company withdraws to Hill 314. Glosters hold positions throughout the day. Night 23/24 April 188 and 189 Divs launch assault on B and C companies who withdraw to Hill 235. Dawn 25 April Glosters surrounded and only D company breaks out.

Chinese thrusts

UN retreat

initial UN deployment

Right: British troops of the Gloucester Regiment dig in, in preparation for the renewed communist offensive across the Imjin River. Far right: US-equipped Belgian forces, in March 1951, shortly before their involvement in the action at the Imjin River.

patrol wading across. The patrol was allowed to approach within easy range before the Glosters opened fire; three of the patrol were killed outright and four more were dragged back to the far bank by their comrades.

There were no further contacts that night but the following day air reconnaissance revealed that the tracks leading south to the Imjin were jammed with marching columns and such transport as the Chinese possessed. Extra ammunition was issued and the battalion prepared for battle. After dusk Carne posted an ambush platoon under Second Lieutenant G. F. B. Temple at the ford to give early warning of the enemy's approach.

By 2230 hours the Chinese had reached Gloster Crossing and begun to wade across. They were met by the sustained fire of Temple's platoon and cut down in the shallow water while artillery and mortar fire inflicted terrible carnage among the packed ranks on the far bank. The platoon held its ground until midnight, by which time its ammunition was exhausted, then doubled back under cover of an artillery strike.

The enemy belonged to the 187th Division, the commander of which, finding himself balked at Gloster Crossing, had sought and found an alternative ford 2km (1½ miles) to the west. Two battalions filed across this and then closed in on A Company's position on Castle Hill, starting a tremendous six-hour struggle for possession of this feature. The battle was fought in bright moonlight, aided by drifting parachute flares, the Chinese displaying exemplary courage in pressing their attacks, while the Glosters showed that combination of dogged determination and controlled firepower that is the British infantryman's traditional hall-

mark. Armed with the bolt-action Lee Enfield rifle which, in various forms, had given good service in both World Wars, each rifleman instinctively went through the drill imposed by his musketry instructors: 'Stay in the aim and count off your rounds . . . eight . . . nine . . . ten . . . insert fresh clip . . . one . . . two . . . three . . . .' The terrible rapid fire was thudding into Peng's battalions and decimating them, just as it had done with Von Kluck's assault columns at Mons in 1914. In addition, the Bren light machine guns were hammering away in three- and four-round bursts, and the belt-fed Vickers were scything through the enemy's ranks. Yet still the Chinese came on, braving shell and mortar bursts, each attack ending in a flurry of exchanged grenades and the rattle of sub-machine guns and pistols. Even as it sank into the ground another attack would be on the way in; in Korea

the expression 'Trigger Fatigue' had a very real meaning.

A Company was fighting odds of 6:1 on Castle Hill, twice that normally required for a successful assault, but was still holding out, although the Castle itself fell after a bitter struggle. At length the Chinese pressure slackened, although an extensive build-up began in front of 2 and 3 Platoons on the forward slopes. Major Angier, the company commander, appreciating that a renewed assault would probably overrun both platoons and reach the summit, organised a first-light counter-attack over the crest by 1 Platoon, led by Lieutenant Philip Curtis. This took the enemy completely by surprise and in the process of forming up, and they suffered severely. Curtis then led an attack on the Castle but was badly wounded by a grenade. His men dragged him to cover but he refused to be restrained and renewed his attack single-handed. He was killed by a burst of machine-gun fire just as he threw his own grenade; this bounced into the bunker, blew the muzzle off the enemy weapon and killed its crew. For his supreme courage and self-sacrifice he was awarded a posthumous Victoria Cross.

Angier and his artillery Forward Observation Officer (FOO) moved into 2 Platoon's position and began directing the guns onto the enemy massed below, with fearful results. However, it was now apparent that while the Chinese had been stopped, A Company no longer possessed sufficient resources to hold Castle Hill. It was ordered to withdraw to Point 235, henceforth known as Gloster Hill. During the early stages of this manoeuvre Angier

and the FOO were killed by machine-gun fire, but Company Sergeant-Major H. Gallagher assumed temporary command and coordinated the platoons' movements. The Chinese did not attempt to interfere and were, in fact, kept pinned to the forward slopes of Castle Hill by a blanket of bursting high explosive. The company's strength was now down to one officer and 53 men.

D Company had fought a similarly ferocious battle throughout the night; at one stage 10 Platoon was overrun, although 12 of its men managed to fight their way clear. At first light Carne ordered this company, too, back to Gloster Hill.

Heading for the high ground

On the Glosters' right flank B Company, although not as severely pressed as A and D, had beaten off several attacks with severe loss to the enemy. Of greater significance was the fact that it had witnessed the Chinese 188th Division ford the Imjin and move into the gap between themselves and the Fusiliers, heading for the high ground on Kamak-San. The company was now in serious danger of being cut off and Carne ordered it to withdraw 1400m (1530yd) to Point 314. This feature was found to be in the possession of Chinese infiltration parties but by 1030 hours these had been disposed of.

During the morning of 23 April the Glosters' F Echelon arrived with food and ammunition and some 40 of the battalion's wounded were evacuated, but at noon the Chinese cut the route to the rear and established a strong roadblock on the

track. Since both his flanks had now been turned as well, Carne could have asked for permission to break out, yet that was not his way. The fact was that the Chinese desperately needed the track, and as far as Carne was concerned they were not going to get it. During the afternoon Brigadier Brodie informed him that an attempt would be made to reinforce the battalion the following day.

The Glosters' stand had already thrown Peng's plans a good 24 hours out of phase, and had reduced the 187th Division to a mere wreck of its former self. The commander of the 63rd Army, under intense pressure to get on, decided to use both the 188th and 189th Divisions in a night attack intended to wipe the stubborn battalion off the map. The attack began at 2230 hours on the 23rd and was directed against B and C Companies. The Chinese seemed unaware of B Company's exact location and advanced obliquely across its front, being shot down in droves as they did so. When they discovered their error they found that their only lines of approach were along steep ridges which had already been designated killing-grounds in the Glosters' defensive fire-plan. Despite their seeming indifference to incurring frightful losses they made little progress. Soon, however, they discovered the gap between B and C Companies and began to penetrate this in large numbers. C Company, on lower ground than B, were clearly vulnerable, and a mass attack which rolled down the slope swamped both 8 and 9 Platoons. A further attack on Company HQ and 7 Platoon was beaten off at 0400 hours, but the serious situation which had now

developed placed Battalion HQ and the mortar positions in the defile below in the direst jeopardy, and Carne moved these onto Gloster Hill, where they were joined by the remnants of C Company.

B Company was now isolated and was ordered to break out at first light, covered by 45 Regiment RA and the fire of the Vickers on Gloster Hill. The operation was extremely difficult since the company was still heavily engaged and the enemy had infiltrated the entire surrounding area. In the event only a 20-strong party under Major Harding managed to reach Gloster Hill; the remainder, with the exception of two men who worked their way south to rejoin the brigade, were captured.

The fight for Gloster Hill

The morning of the 24th, therefore, found Carne's battalion and its attached personnel, now numbering less than 400 effectives, concentrated on Gloster Hill, still acting as a cork to the bottleneck entrance of the Solma-ri defile. The relief force, consisting of a Filipino infantry combat team with a troop of M24

Chaffee light tanks and part of C Squadron 8th Hussars, managed to reach the old F Echelon area, which lay 6km (4 miles) south of the battalion's position. However, in the defile beyond, one of the light tanks which was leading the advance was hit by bazooka fire and set ablaze, blocking all further progress forward, and the attempt was abandoned.

Carne was nonetheless determined to hold out. Water was in short supply and most was reserved for the wounded. There were too few Brens remaining and ammunition was running low. Most serious of all was the fact that only 10–15 hours of life remained in the batteries powering the battalion's radios, without which the lifeline to the guns would be lost. Major Digby Grist, the Glosters' second-in-command and commander of the Left Out of Battle Party, was well aware of the situation and at dusk organised a supply drop with 15 Sentinel light aircraft from which several boxes of ammunition were recovered. Carne also received the encouraging news that ground-attack aircraft, hitherto fully engaged elsewhere, would be available for his support the following day.

Above: Chinese infantry on the attack. The Chinese were a formidable foe. Not only did they show a disregard for casualties that made it difficult to cope with their assaults, they also proved themselves past masters at the art of infiltrating positions at night, shattering the morale of the defenders. Below: The aftermath of the Imjin River. Those Glosters who survived the ordeal on Hill 235 attend the final roll call.

After dusk he pulled in his perimeter to the summit of the hill so that the first enemy attacks, which began at 2200 hours, struck empty space. Once more, the battle raged throughout the night, the Chinese demonstrating that they had learned nothing from their previous experience. Carne was the soul of the defence and twice, armed with a rifle and grenades, he personally routed parties of the enemy who had penetrated the defences. His conduct earned him not only the Victoria Cross but also the American Distinguished Service Cross.

As the light began to strengthen the Chinese began to mass for their final attack and could be seen in their hundreds on the slopes of the hill. Their bugles struck a jarring, triumphant note and Carne's adjutant, Captain Anthony Farrar-Hockley, suggested that the Glosters' own bugles should answer them. Only one, that belonging to Drummer Eagles, remained to the battalion, but this was used to good effect by Staff-Sergeant Buss, the Drum-Major. Disdaining cover, Buss stood up in his slit trench and began with the *Long Reveille,* then blew every call in the book with the exception of *Retreat,* the notes rolling defiantly around the battle-scarred Imjin hills. Seven times during the next hour the enemy closed in for the kill, and each time they were pitched back down the hill.

At 0830 hours on 25 April the last radio battery died and the all-important link with the guns was severed. Even had the link survived, the 25-pounders would

have been unable to provide further support for a while, since the enemy's infiltration parties had penetrated so far south that the gun lines were already under smallarms fire, and 45 Regiment RA was having to limber-up and retire to fresh positions.

Fortune, however, does sometimes favour the brave, for at this precise moment the long-awaited air support arrived in the form of a flight of Lockheed

F-80 Shooting Stars. Observing the smoke marker rising from the Glosters' position, they howled in to the attack, napalm drop-tanks tumbling to burst in gigantic fireballs in the packed ranks of the Chinese, burning away the scrub in which they lay concealed. Then the jets raked the slopes with cannon-fire. A dozen more Shooting Stars swept in shortly after to strafe between the hill and the river.

A period of comparative calm des-

Left: Royal Artillery 25-pounder guns in action. The 25-pounder was one of the most effective field guns in the world during this period, and was a great strength of the British Army. Above: Victims of UN artillery – despite taking shelter in this gully, these communist troops found there was no escape from accurate bombardment and air-bursting shells.

Once the communist offensive had been held, then the UN forces could counterattack. Below: US troops move forward in May. Above: Men of the King's Own Scottish Borderers pass a Centurion tank while on patrol north of the Imjin River, 10 June 1951. Opposite page: US infantrymen of the 35th Infantry Regiment hitch lifts on Sherman tanks as they prepare for action on the west central front.

cended on the flame-girdled hill, disturbed only by machine-gun fire from the surrounding features. Carne had received permission to break out at 0605 hours on the 26th and, knowing that his battalion had fought its fight and could do no more, he used the lull to organise attempts by the survivors to work their way back to the UN lines. Eagles, recognising that the chances of success were very slim indeed, blew his bugle apart with a grenade rather than have it fall into the enemy's hands. The wounded had to be left behind in the care of the Medical Officer, Captain R. P. Hickey, and the Chaplain, Captain the Rev. S. J. Davies, and their helpers, and these men were still performing their tasks when the Chinese finally crept warily onto the summit of Gloster Hill.

Of the rest, only a handful escaped capture, Carne himself being among the last to be taken. A total of 58 Glosters had been killed during the three-day battle, and a further 30 died during their cruel captivity. Only 63 men, the majority from D Company, reached safety, and with these and the personnel of A, B and F Echelons Major Grist began reconstructing the battalion. Throughout the next day Glosters came in from instructional courses, hospital and local leave in Japan, and soon after the first reinforcements had arrived a signal was sent to the regiment's colonel-in-chief, HRH The Duke of Gloucester, that the 1st Battalion was operational again. Ridgway and Van Fleet both sent letters of commendation to Grist, Van Fleet subsequently adding that the Glosters' action had provided 'the most outstanding example of unit bravery in modern warfare'. On 8 May the 1st Battalion, the Gloucestershire Regiment, and C Troop, 170 Independent Mortar Battery were honoured with a US Presidential Citation which did full justice to their magnificent achievement.

The remainder of the 29th Brigade had fought an equally epic battle. The Belgian battalion across the river had been hard-hit but had held its ground and then successfully withdrawn during the night of 23/24 April, the move covered by a US tank battalion on the brigade's right flank and by the fire of the Royal Ulster Rifles, who had moved forward to

occupy a position on the right of the Royal Northumberland Fusiliers. Throughout the 24th the Chinese, balked by the Glosters at Solma-ri, made frantic efforts to secure the secondary track running through the brigade's position. These attacks were, as usual, made regardless of loss and made little progress, although the enemy did succeed in turning the brigade's flanks. At 1030 hours on 25 April Brodie received orders to extract his command and conform to the general withdrawal being executed by I Corps. This was far easier said than done, for shortly afterwards the enemy established themselves astride the track leading to the rear.

Armoured Support

There can be little doubt that had it not been for the Centurion tanks of C Squadron, King's Royal Irish Hussars, commanded by Major Henry Huth, the brigade would have sustained far more serious casualties than it did. During this episode, one of the bloodiest of the entire battle, tank commanders fought at a

distinct disadvantage; poor visibility and bad going meant that they could only operate with maximum efficiency if their hatches were open, yet the enemy's use of mortars and his willingness to come to close quarters demanded that they remained closed down. After fighting their way through a serious ambush on the way forward the Hussars provided covering fire while first the Fusiliers and then one company of the Ulster Rifles broke contact. It then became apparent that the Chinese were tightening their grip on the track to the rear, and all but one of the remaining Ulster Rifles companies struck across the hills on a parallel route. With the tanks acting as rearguard the Belgians and the last Ulster Rifles company conducted a fighting withdrawal through the valley. The Chinese were now swarming all over the hills and, displaying insane courage, repeatedly tried to smother the Centurions with their human-wave tactics. Great swathes were cut through their ranks by the 20-pounders and the co-axial machine guns, but still they clambered aboard and attempted to pry open the hatches, to be shot off time

and again by the fire of other tanks; one commander swept his vehicle clean of the enemy by driving straight through a house. During the worst phase of the withdrawal the tanks were forced to run a gauntlet of fire 2km (1½ miles) in length, the injured and exhausted infantrymen riding on their decks suffering terribly. Several of the Centurions which reached safety were piled high with dead and wounded, their sides running scarlet with blood; there was blood on the tracks, too, but none of that was British or Belgian. The Chinese continued to press C Squadron closely until the new UN line was reached. Five tanks had been lost, three through enemy action and two because of the atrocious going; all were promptly destroyed by gunfire to prevent them being used by the enemy.

With this incident ended the Battle of the Imjin River. The 29th Brigade had lost a quarter of its men but was still a fighting entity. The Chinese 63rd Army, however, was not. It had sustained 11,000 casualties, over 40% of its combat strength, and that same day orders were issued for it to be pulled out of the line.

It returned to China and took no further part in the war.

So much had depended upon the 63rd Army that Peng's strategy now lay in ruins. Van Fleet had used the delay imposed on the enemy at the Imjin to establish what he called the 'No Name Line' some kilometres north of Seoul, and this easily absorbed the enemy's weakened attempts to break through. By the end of April the offensive had clearly failed, the cost to the communists being 70,000 casualties, while the UN losses were only one-tenth of that figure.

Typically, Peng was unable to accept the situation, and on 15 May he launched a fresh offensive with 21 Chinese and nine North Korean divisions, aimed at X Corps and the ROK III Corps. The latter was routed, as it had been on every previous occasion when attacked, and the enemy effected a penetration some 50km (30 miles) deep. On the right of this the more experienced ROK I Corps estab-

lished a hard shoulder but on the left two X Corps formations, the ROK 5th and 7th Divisions, were forced to give way after a hard fight. This in turn exposed the right flank of the US 2nd Division which, in spite of sustaining 900 casualties, stood firm and inflicted an estimated 35,000 on the Chinese; as evidence of the Van Fleet Load in action, one of the division's field artillery battalions fired no less than 12,000 rounds of 105mm ammunition in one 24-hour period.

Van Fleet had correctly assessed the area in which Peng's blow would fall and had already established a strategic reserve with the US 3rd Division and the 187th Airborne Regiment, the former moving quickly forward to secure the open flank of the 2nd Division while a series of counterattacks began against the western edge of the communist salient.

Once more the Eighth Army 'rolled with the punch', trading ground for Chinese lives. By 20 May the communists

had again outrun their over-extended supply line and in a week's fighting had incurred a staggering 90,000 casualties.

On 22 May Van Fleet began a counter-offensive along the entire length of the front, omitting the unreliable ROK III Corps from his order of battle. On the extreme right the ROK I Corps advanced straight up the coast against negligible opposition to seize Kansong. In the centre progress was a little slower but by 24 May the 187th Airborne Regiment and the 1st Marine Division had reached the Hwachon Reservoir and Inje. On the left I Corps reoccupied its old positions on the Imjin.

The official US Marine Corps History has succinctly described what followed:

Only from the air could the effects of the UN counterstroke of May and June 1951 be fully appreciated. It was more than a CCF withdrawal: it was a flight of beaten troops under very little control in some instances. They were

As the UN offensive pushed the communists back in May and June, so US mobility and firepower came into its own. Above: US Rangers break cover as they push across the 38th Parallel in June 1951. Left: A rather studiously posed photograph of members of the 65th Regimental Combat Team. Right above: US advisers with the ROK 15th Regiment which moved up with the US forces. Right: US paratroops, used in May 1951 to try to cut the Chinese lines of retreat, scatter under a rain of mortar fire.

scourged with bullets, rockets, and napalm as planes swooped down on them like hawks scattering chickens. And where it had been rare for a single Chinese soldier to surrender voluntarily, remnants of platoons, companies and even battalions were now giving up after throwing down their arms.

There had been nothing like it before, and its like would never be seen in Korea again. The enemy was on the run!

At this point the president and his Joint Chiefs of Staff forbade a general pursuit to the north. This directive was the subject of intense discussion between the State Department and the Defense Department. There were sound military reasons for not maintaining the UN advance as far as the Yalu River. As Ridgway put it: 'It would not have been worth the cost. It would have widened our battle-front from 110 miles to 420. We stopped on what I believe to be the strongest line on our immediate front.'

The talks begin

Van Fleet was, however, permitted to secure limited objectives with a view to consolidating his overall position, and he pursued this policy throughout the first half of June, mounting Operation Piledriver with I and IX Corps to capture Chorwon and Kumwha, the southern points of the Iron Triangle, while X Corps

cleaned out the Punch Bowl north of Sowha, another fortified zone which the communists had previously used as a springboard for their offensives. His successes gave the UN forces the advantage of the dominant positions for the rest of the war.

It was now apparent even to the most dedicated communist that the terribly mauled Chinese Red Army was incapable of defeating the United Nations in the field. In China itself the war was far from being universally popular and the government was forced to adopt a policy of brutal repression to stifle criticism. The Chinese economy was quite unable to support the burden, which was largely carried by Soviet Russia, with serious financial consequences for the entire communist bloc. The time had obviously come when further pursuit of the Korean adventure was regarded as being counterproductive, for on 23 June the Soviet delegate to the United Nations proposed a ceasefire. Delegates from both sides met at the village of Kaesong the following month. But it was to be two more years before the war was ended.

8. The Communist Forces

Although they shared some of the same characteristics the Chinese and North Korean forces were as different as chalk and cheese. These differences in equipment, ideology and fighting methods varied in degree according to the amount of influence that the Soviet Union was able to exert on each side of the communist allies. The contrast between the tactics used in the opening North Korean offensive of June 1950 and the entry of the Chinese Communist Forces (CCF) into the fighting in October was very marked. As the war progressed and Russian doctrines became more accepted by the Chinese, the differences lessened but never vanished.

The surprising part of this contrast was that the backbone of the Korean People's Army (KPA) was composed of veterans from the Chinese People's Liberation Army (CPLA). When the KPA launched

its invasion of the South it had a strength of ten regular divisions and five brigades of border constabulary. Although the border constabulary had been recruited from Koreans who had fled to Soviet territory during the Japanese occupation, it was a different story with the army. The 5th and 6th Divisions were Korean divisions of the CPLA which had simply been transferred to North Korean control. The 7th Division was made up of Koreans combed out of other CPLA formations, while the 1st and 4th Divisions each contained a regiment of Korean CPLA veterans. The KPA therefore had a large proportion of experienced men trained in the Chinese communist tradition of warfare.

Although the Korean leader Kim Il Sung was happy to use men who had fought in the CPLA he was more impressed by Soviet military organisation.

As a result the KPA was trained by Soviet advisers and had a much more lavish scale of equipment than its veteran soldiers had been used to in the CPLA. Indeed it was the equipment that was the key to KPA tactical doctrine. As usual there was a typically Russian reliance on powerful artillery, and each division had field

Opposite page above: Communist prisoners, taken at the Battle of Pork Chop Hill. Opposite page below: To the accompaniment of martial music, Chinese troops cross the Yalu. Left: A wounded Chinese soldier captured in February 1951. Below: A KPA officer in Kaesong, July 1951.

artillery, medium artillery and even 12 SU-76 self-propelled guns, but the main battle-winning weapon was the tank force of 120 T34s. By the standards of northeast Asia the KPA was a modern force trained to engage in the sort of combat that had been typical of the European theatre in World War II. It was effective too and its bold use of tanks quickly drove the South Korean and US forces down the Korean peninsula to their last stronghold at Pusan. This edge over its opponents in equipment was necessarily short-lived once the Americans recovered from the shock of the invasion and delivered their sensational counter-blow at Inchon.

Allies and advisers

In the fortnight after the landings at Inchon on 15 September 1950 the KPA was virtually destroyed, and had to be rebuilt behind the shield of the CCF. Despite the fact that the Chinese intervention had saved them from total defeat, the North Koreans still preferred to rely on Russian advisers and still remained a force patterned on the Soviet model. Although the bulk of the fighting was carried out by the Chinese, the KPA gradually recuperated from the disaster of September 1950 to number its original strength of ten divisions by the end of the war in July 1953. During this time KPA soldiers continued to earn the respect of their opponents for their toughness and their incredible courage, which bordered on the fanatical.

There is no doubt that part of the secret of the KPA's survival in the face of

disaster was the success of its political indoctrination programme. The Korean Communist Party had absorbed the lessons taught by its Soviet mentor and established complete control of the army at every level. There was a political officer or commissar for each army, division, regiment, battalion and company. In each company there was a Party cell which was composed of the platoon commanders and selected NCOs and soldiers. As 20% of even the most junior ranks were

reckoned to be Party members, the very smallest unit had a sprinkling of politically motivated men. All commanders of field rank and above had a commissar at their elbow, which must have been a great cement to their loyalty when things went badly. At the company and battalion level the Party techniques of political education and discussion were used with some success: even the teaching of slogans produces some effect – if only a limited one.

This indoctrination had a patchy effect which produced rather contradictory performances. The North Koreans were obviously very confident of its powers because they had no hesitation in releasing some 50,000 South Korean prisoners-of-war in the autumn of 1951 and promptly conscripting them into the KPA. The control of the KPA by the Communist Party organisation meant that these recruits, who were almost certainly unwilling, would be watched and subjected to constant political pressure. Once away from this organised coercion KPA soldiers were by no means entirely reliable. The oddest illustration of this came from the prison camps in which captured KPA men were held by the United Nations. Political organisation in the camps was still strong and the prisoners were able to embarrass their captors by organising a number of bloody riots and by showing an extraordinary degree of intransigence. Yet when these same hostile prisoners were screened by the United Nations before repatriation some 20,000 of the approximately 90,000 North Koreans did not wish to be sent home. Once away from the rigid discipline imposed by the Party nearly a quarter of North Koreans showed that they had been unimpressed by its political indoctrination.

No return

When the same screening process was tried on the 20,000 prisoners from the CCF there were even more dismal results for communism, with only 6400 electing to return to China. There is no doubt that this was a great surprise to the United Nations because the CCF had established an awesome reputation for hardiness and fanatical courage. The lower morale among Chinese prisoners may have been a reflection of the fact that the CCF had been even more roughly handled than the KPA in terms of casualties suffered, and had a much more marked inferiority in equipment and technique to its opponents.

The most remarkable achievement of the CCF was that it managed any success at all in the face of UN firepower. Its initial offensive owed much to surprise but also to an element of confusion because everything about the CCF was different to the KPA. To start with it was obvious that the KPA had been long and deliberately prepared for the invasion of the South. The CCF, on the other hand, was so ill-equipped to take on the forces against it that it appeared to have been rushed into the struggle as an emergency measure to forestall the total defeat of communist forces in Korea. The difference in weapon types used by the two armies is significant enough. The KPA was thoroughly equipped with Russian arms but the CCF had a baffling assortment of weapons, including Russian PPSh 'burp guns', US and British arms captured from the Nationalist Chinese, and weapons taken from the Japanese in World War II.

The reason for this contrast was that the CCF, also known as the Chinese People's Volunteers (CPV), did not consist of 'volunteers' at all but was made up of units of the CCF drafted hurriedly to Korea. Far from being equipped by the Soviet Union, the CCF had fought and won China's long civil war without any material help from the Russians. Naturally enough the Chinese were forced to rely on the tactics which had brought success against the Nationalists even though their enemies in the Korean theatre were so superior in organisation and weapons.

Satchels and burp guns

To face the modern army of the United Nations there were six Chinese armies each composed of three divisions of some 10,000 men. For artillery each division had a mere battalion of pack weapons and there were no tanks or towed guns. To combat enemy tanks the Chinese had to rely on TNT satchel charges which were in reality no defence at all. The only standard personal weapon was the 'burp gun', but assorted rifles, carbines, pistols and sub-machine guns were common. The lack of heavy equipment meant that CCF units were able to move stealthily across country, which was just as well considering the overwhelming US air superiority. All Chinese troop movements took place at night, which gave them the advantage of surprise on a number of occasions, but also helped them to avoid the attentions of hostile planes.

The CCF also made a virtue out of necessity in requiring only a tiny administrative 'tail'. A Chinese division could function on 40 tonnes of rations, water, clothing, ammunition and fuel a day while a comparable number of UN troops needed 350 tonnes a day. CCF soldiers carried most of their immediate requirements with them: a personal weapon, 80 rounds of ammunition, grenades, ammunition for automatic weapons and either mortar bombs or a TNT satchel charge. Each man carried emergency rations of rice and pulses, tea and salt for five days. The soldiers were expected to supplement this austere diet with locally obtained vegetables or captured rations but there was not always much opportunity for scavenging in Korea.

Although the CCF needed so much less than the UN forces it found it hard enough to supply even these basic wants.

For political reasons UN aircraft did not operate across the Chinese border, so supplies could be brought that far with comparative ease. Once across the border, lack of motor transport meant that the CCF's main supply line was the railway. This was, naturally, much bombed and had to be constantly repaired at night by gangs of workers stationed along the line. The rest of the Chinese supplies travelled forward in the most primitive way imaginable – by porter. Thousands of peasants shouldering around 40kg (88lb) in bamboo baskets and moving only at night were the CCF's umbilical cord. The degree of organisation and effort required to supply the front-line troops for an offensive was phenomenal and they never really had the luxury of copious provisions. Indeed the intensity of a Chinese offensive tended to fade after five or six days when supplies ran low, and there was usually an enforced pause while restocking took place.

To others these disadvantages might have been crippling but the Chinese had long been accustomed to them in fighting the Nationalists and had evolved tactics which were especially suited to the situation. Relying so greatly on a massed and

Opposite page: A curious US soldier examines the inside of a T34/85. Top: Chinese infantry on the march. Above: Lin Piao, veteran of the Chinese civil war and the commander of the Chinese forces that conducted the initial offensive in Korea.

Above: KPA forces were well equipped to endure the cold of the Korean winter in the first stages of the war, with quilted outer clothing and well designed caps. Below: US troops move in after riots in POW camps in South Korea. Tear gas was used to disperse and control the rioting North Korean prisoners. Opposite page: A good side view of one of the most successful weapons systems of the 20th century, the T34/85 tank. This was the mainstay of the Chinese and KPA armoured units.

disciplined human effort meant that they were expert in moving very large numbers of men in great secrecy. Lack of motor vehicles meant that they were not tied to the roads so they could position and supply forces in places where their more heavily equipped enemies were weak. Their strengths were mobility, deception and surprise, which enabled them to concentrate rapidly to deliver an unexpected attack. Their favoured method of attack was to surround an enemy unit or at least assault it from two sides and they were prepared to pay a very heavy cost in casualties for important positions.

Bugles, whistles and flags

All these characteristics made an attack by the CCF very distinctive. It was sudden, it usually seemed to involve very large numbers and it was noisy. Because signalling in the CCF was so primitive (there was one communications company to a division and there were no radios below regimental level) command in battle was maintained by bugle calls, whistles and flags. This pandemonium had a psychological value in unnerving an enemy but it was inferior as a means of communication. The difficulty of controlling troops on the battlefield was one reason why the Chinese tended to attack

in closely packed formations, a tactic which became known as the 'human-wave' assault. Against the firepower deployed by UN troops these tactics were very costly, and damaging even for an army with the manpower resources of the Chinese.

As a result of all these material disadvantages the morale of the CCF began to suffer when it was pushed back by the UN forces. The first reverses came in the bitter winter weather of early 1951. Although the Chinese had experience of the harsh climate of the region they had many casualties from frostbite. Their medical support was hard-pressed, with only one company to a division, and was unable to prevent an outbreak of typhoid. The individual Chinese soldier was a sturdy individual who seemed, to his Western opponents, to exhibit superhuman qualities of stoicism and endurance, but he had a limit.

By the middle of 1951 the CCF had been through quite an ordeal. Whenever it made contact with its enemies, in victory or defeat, it had the disadvantage of suffering heavy casualties in the face of their firepower. Its supply at all times was an immense labour and it operated under the continuous threat of UN air power. In general the technical advantages of the UN forces were so great that the Chinese

found it impossible to stop them when they had the initiative. The circumstances were depressing and the UN did not neglect the opportunity for psychological warfare. Leaflets and safe-conduct passes were dropped among the communists.

The Chinese commanders took steps to counteract the sag in morale. Units which had taken heavy punishment were broken up, their personnel disbanded and sent to other units in accordance with the established custom of the CCF. This practice was intended to prevent defeated units becoming demoralised, but it was the very opposite of traditional military thinking. In Western countries a depleted unit would be made up to strength with reinforcements. The CCF also withdrew ahead of the somewhat ponderous advance of UN forces in order to escape the attrition of battle against their superior weaponry. Most remarkably of all, the Chinese changed their military philosophy because they realised that, in Korea, they lacked the room for manoeuvre and support from the rural population which had helped them to succeed against the Nationalists. They drew the correct conclusions and began to espouse Soviet military methods.

It was not possible to change the lightly equipped but highly mobile Chinese forces into a modern well-armed army very quickly. The Soviet Union may have had difficulties managing to provide weaponry on such a large scale and probably also had reservations about the wisdom of creating a powerful Chinese army. One way and another the CCF began to enjoy more material support, particularly in the matter of artillery, but it was never able to equal the firepower of the UN forces. By the end of the war it had changed very greatly, resembling a model of the Soviet army with a reduced equipment scale, which made it much the same sort of organisation as the KPA.

Joint command

On the surface relations between the KPA and the CCF were harmonious enough. Command from a joint HQ was nominally exercised by Kim Il Sung although the Chinese were obviously the senior partner of the two communist combatant nations and Russian influence was always very strong. There is no reason to suppose that there was any real friction between these allies during the years that the war lasted; but this easy collaboration was a surprising achievement because both Chinese and North Korean communists had embarked on extreme cults based on the personalities of their leaders. KPA Orders of the Day betrayed an almost comical reverence for the person of the great leader, Kim Il Sung, and made ornate declarations of the immense love and loyalty owed to him by his devoted soldiers. The frantic, virtual worship of Mao Tse-tung by the Chinese was then in its infancy, but the personality of the Party chairman was an important element in Chinese political indoctrination. The result of this stress on Party leaders was that Korean and Chinese communists maintained a separate identity even as they engaged in a common struggle and even as their armed forces became more similar, and more Soviet, in character.

Despite the difficulties, the KPA trod the path between Chinese and Russian influence very surely. Principally this was because the KPA was not master of its own fate but relied on the other communist powers for its very existence: the Soviets provided equipment and the Chinese provided manpower. The whole point of the KPA's existence was to unify Korea by force and it was happy to accept help from any source to achieve this. A hardheaded realisation that North Korean forces alone had no chance of winning the struggle reconciled them to accepting the direction of their communist allies and made for a cooperation that appeared to be without friction.

9. The Long Stalemate

On 23 June 1951 Jacob Malik, Soviet delegate to the United Nations, made a proposal for discussions between the belligerents in Korea. Two days later a Chinese newspaper, the *People's Daily*, endorsed Malik's proposal and, with the aid of much diplomatic manoeuvring, it was agreed that ceasefire negotiations should take place in the town of Kaesong. The first session on 10 July was totally unsatisfactory from the UN point of view: it emerged that the town of Kaesong, far from being on neutral territory, was firmly in communist hands, which enabled them to make various propaganda points to the effect that the UN delegation was there to negotiate a surrender rather than discuss a ceasefire. It also seemed to the American negotiators that the communist attitude was totally unrealistic and more geared to scoring propaganda points than achieving agreement. This opinion was strengthened when the talks were broken off after the communists alleged that the UN forces had tried to murder their delegation by air attack on 22 August.

By this time reinforcements had made General Van Fleet's forces more powerful than ever and he was allowed to renew his offensive. One of his most important objectives was to drive the Chinese Communist Forces (CCF) and Korean People's Army (KPA) back from the Hwachon Reservoir which not only supplied water to the Korean capital of Seoul but also provided its electricity. This task was much more difficult now that the communists had enjoyed a short breathing space to re-equip – most notably with quantities of new artillery. The Bloody Ridge/Heartbreak Ridge complex changed hands a number of times in heavy fighting between August and October but was finally taken by the US 2nd Infantry Division on 14 October. Further west the UN forces had pushed on to objectives up to 30km (19 miles) north of the 38th parallel. During this dour struggle the communist casualties had once again been very great while their forces were manifestly going backwards, so there was military pressure on them to resume negotiations.

The communist proposal on 7 October that the conference be resumed at the more suitable site of Panmunjom, 8km (5 miles) east of Kaesong and genuinely in no-man's-land, may well have been forced by the deteriorating military situation. Whether that was so or not, the talks were resumed at Panmunjom on 25 October and, within a few weeks, the UN side had made a very serious tactical error. Van Fleet had been ordered to cease major offensive action on 12 November and to confine his forces to an active defence of their front line, which was to be known from that moment on as the Main Line of Resistance (MLR). From that time onwards Van Fleet was forbidden to mount an attack of greater than battalion size without the express permis-

sion of the UN Commander-in-Chief, General Ridgway. Conscious that the UN forces were no longer looking for territorial gains and were desperate for an end to the war, the UN Command made a Washington-inspired proposal that the current contact line should represent the final demarcation line provided an armistice was signed within 30 days of an agreement on the proposal.

A frozen front line

Of course the latest UN move contained an implied threat: if there was no armistice their forces might well resume the offensive. More importantly it offered tne communists the certainty that, for 30 days at least, the UN would not make a major attack. They hastened to ratify the proposal on 27 November but made no serious effort to conclude an armistice agreement by 27 December. By that time they had gained a 30-day *de facto* ceasefire, free from the pressure of Van Fleet's forces, and they used it well. In that time a frenzied digging and tunnelling effort transformed their lines into an almost impregnable fortification. Thus the situation on the ground in Korea was frozen into something very close to the shape it

would bear at the end of the struggle nearly two years later.

Stretching 250km (155 miles) across the peninsula of Korea the MLRs of the two sides were fashioned for a static war that reflected their different strengths and weaknesses. The communists were forced to use the reverse slopes of the hills they held by their inferiority in firepower. Into these reverse slopes, safe from the expertly handled UN artillery, they dug warrens of tunnels and caves to house their army of 850,000 men. The overhead protection of the communist forces was so

Opposite page: Colonel Chang Chun San of the North Korean delegation at the ceasefire negotiations, initials one of the maps over which the long and complicated debates took place. For two years there was stalemated fighting and bitter discussion as the talks dragged on. Below: Digging in to hold the line. The UN troops were able to construct a shallower defensive system than that of the communists because of their more effective artillery support, but this still involved much spadework for the infantry. Bottom: Trudging up to the front in the summer heat.

thick that it was evidently designed to withstand even nuclear attack, and their posts were constructed in a fortified belt that was 25–40km (15–25 miles) deep. While these positions were obviously very strong defensively they had disadvantages for any commander who wished to take the offensive. The artillery for instance was so deeply dug-in that it would not have been easy to take it forward.

In contrast to the communist effort the UN MLR was much less substantial. Because of the weight of UN firepower it took the form of a simple trench and bunker line slashed into the forward slopes of the UN-held hill crests. To provide some sort of cushion in front of the MLR itself, there were a number of fortified outposts at some distance forward of the line which made the most of any features in the rugged Korean topography. In contrast to the enormous trench systems of the Western Front in World War I, there was little behind the UN MLR in terms of support or reserve trenches. The superior

manoeuvrability of a modern army meant that reserves could be rushed very quickly to any possible breakthrough and, as a result, could be maintained in more comfort at some distance behind the line until needed.

The disadvantage of the UN positions was that they were so shallow. At any time a determined and sudden Chinese attack could push UN troops off a feature which was vital to the integrity of the MLR. In response the UN Command could use all the superior weaponry available to it to help its forces regain the lost feature but no amount of machinery and high explosive could prevent casualties among the counterattacking infantry. This situation gave rise to the numerous bloody little battles of position which formed the only major actions of the stalemated war, and which put the colourfully named features of 'Jane Russell Hill', 'White Horse Hill' and 'Luke the Gook's Castle' into the military lexicon.

In this dispiriting position it was the

Above left: The debris of war litters a Korean hillside as US troops take a break after a successful offensive against a hill-top position. Above: Constant care and maintenance of weapons was one of the essential routine tasks of the US infantryman. Above right: Under camouflage netting, US gunners prepare a howitzer for action.

the UN air force could destroy inland communications. By the end of June (long before Van Fleet's forces had reached the eventual MLR) much UN air power had been switched from close-support operations to the interdiction bombing dictated by Operation Strangle.

It was known that the communications problems of the communist forces had been greatly eased by the introduction of huge numbers of Soviet-supplied trucks in 1951. Indeed the number of trucks available to them was believed to have risen from 7300 in January to something over 55,000 by June. If the UN Command could destroy the eight highways which led south to the front line from the secure railheads in Chinese Manchuria, the fleet of trucks would be unable to get the supplies through. From the end of June and throughout July UN aircraft of all types carried out an assault on the North Korean road system, cratering the road beds, destroying bridges and passes, firing rockets into tunnels and dropping delayed-action bombs on road junctions. The air sorties continued at night when the lorry convoys used the cover of darkness to move along the highways.

In the face of the striking power of 700 sorties a day the North Korean Department of Military Highway Administration performed brilliantly in keeping the supplies moving. With a force of 20,000 men and liberal conscription of local labour the near-impossible was achieved. The damage of each day was usually repaired within a few hours after dark and the convoys proved very successful at remaining undetected by enemy aircraft at night. The communists were also adept at the arts of concealment and deception. In daylight hours trucks were hidden in caves or disguised as native huts. By August the UN pilots made the gloomy assessment that the volume of trucks using the vital highways had not decreased much as a result of their campaign.

At this time UN intelligence indicated that the North Korean railway system was possibly even more important for the supply of the front than the roads. The lorries were hampered by the fact that they used scarce diesel fuel imported from China, but the railways ran on coal, of which North Korea had a plentiful supply.

communists who held the better hand. The morale problem of their forces had greatly lessened once the front had been stabilised, and their resources of man-power were inexhaustible. In addition to this the communist rulers were unworried by high casualties while the leaders of democracies had to account to public opinion for the loss of life in a distant part of the globe. All this gave rise to some hopes that the UN countries might become sickened by the endless contest and their governments be forced to make a disadvantageous peace settlement. Even while they waited for this moment there were considerable advantages for the communists while the war dragged on. For Stalin the commitment of so many US and European troops in Korea weakened the Central European Front which his forces threatened. For the Chinese the task of resisting an external threat encouraged national cohesiveness at a time when they were making every effort to consolidate the gains of their revolution.

The UN countries, dreading further casualties and longing for a settlement, were at a disadvantage politically and militarily.

Pressure to negotiate

It was obvious enough that the UN Command would have to put the communists under military pressure to make them negotiate in a meaningful way. The strong Chinese defensive positions and the UN's unwillingness to incur great loss of life virtually precluded any major action by ground forces, but there were other options. Korea was a peninsula, which meant that its coasts could be successfully blockaded. The UN navies achieved this despite extensive communist mine warfare and coastal battery fire. While the navies interdicted coastal movement and brought communist forces under bombardment for several kilometres inland, it seemed that the entire front line could be starved of supplies if

Of course the railways did not run right up to the MLR but they possessed a large load-hauling capacity and could bring supplies as far south as the termini at Pyonggang and Sariwon. From August onwards Operation Strangle continued with fierce air force attacks on the railways as well as the roads. The North Korean Railroad Recovery Bureau deployed 18,000 men to meet the onslaught with ant-like industry. As on the roads, railside gangs laboured at night to repair the damage, and a strong emphasis was placed on deception. During the day much rolling stock was hidden in Korea's extensive tunnel system or, if left on the lines in full view, it was apparently wrecked, with its wheels removed, only to be swiftly re-assembled at nightfall. Dummy trains to draw the fire of the UN air force were also deployed with great success. By using every resource the railway system held out.

It was apparent by the time General Mark Clark took over from General Ridgway in May 1952 that Operation Strangle was not succeeding. An alternative approach to crushing the communists by bombing was needed, and in June the Special Targets System was put into action. This involved using large numbers of bombers to eliminate, one by one, targets of major economic or military importance. The programme began with

an attack by 500 aircraft on the Suiho Hydro Dam, which was the fourth largest in the world and supplied electricity to Manchuria as well as most of North Korea. Pyongyang came under sustained bombardment in July and after that oil refineries and industrial sites throughout the country were bombed. The results appeared to be negligible. Repair work was put in hand with astonishing speed and the communist negotiators at Panmunjom gave no indication that they were under any increased pressure. In any case North Korea contained very few

targets of high enough value to suit such a policy.

By the autumn of 1952 the air war had produced so little effect that the communists were able to mount a series of major offensives on the ground. The military forces on both sides had become steadily stronger over the months since Van Fleet's offensive had gained the MLR. By the end of 1952 the communist forces would number 1,200,000, of which one million were Chinese. There were seven Chinese armies and two North Korean corps – some 270,000 soldiers – in

the forward area of the MLR. In support there were 531,000 troops in a further 11 Chinese armies and one North Korean corps, and the remainder of the forces looked after the logistics and supply of the battlefront. The bulk of the line was in the hands of the Chinese, while the North Korean forces spent this stalemated part of the war on the east of the trench line, where they faced South Korean troops.

Manning the MLR

Over the same period the UN forces rose to a total of 768,000 including logistics troops. The fighting element of these was grouped in 16 divisions in the MLR. The components of this group were 11 Republic of Korea (ROK) divisions, one British Commonwealth Division, one US Marine Division and three US Army divisions. In the reserve there were three US Army divisions and one ROK division. All the troops from other UN countries were attached in their various battalions and brigades to the US Army troops and a regiment of ROK Marines was attached to the US Marines. A very large number of US troops (well over 200,000) had been engaged in the conflict since the MLR had been established and their numbers were increased further with the arrival of the first National Guard division at the end of 1951. Naturally

enough much care was taken to maintain the morale of these troops who were fighting for a dimly perceived cause far from home.

As much attention as possible was paid to the material comforts of the soldiers who manned the MLR. The installation of hot showers and a frequent mail delivery made the front line unusually luxurious and the introduction of a helicopter evacuation service for the wounded was considered to be of great importance. There was also a concept of limited service which was new to wartime. In the ordinary way units which had been in action were relieved or taken into the reserve for a rest and refit and, in addition, the soldiers within each unit were constantly changed. The Americans

operated a rotation system which meant that each man returned home after a single combat tour, which lasted between nine months and a year. During their tour US soldiers were flown at least once to Japan for a short recreational leave. The other UN troops were usually treated in much the same way as the Americans – except for the ROK forces. ROK soldiers did not have a limited combat tour and they were often under-equipped and poorly supplied to the point of being ill-fed. However, ROK soldiers were spurred on by the motive of defending their country and their combat performance improved throughout the war. The measures taken to provide the non-Korean UN troops with an unusually high battlefield standard of living also seemed to pay dividends, as morale remained high and the attitude was one of professional pride in soldiering.

Despite the extraordinary facilities of the MLR, life in it could never be really comfortable. The Korean climate is a harsh one and a bitter winter alternates with the great heat of the summer and the muddy downpour of July and August. Besides which, trench warfare is hard work for frontline soldiers. Information from patrols and from prisoners taken in raids is essential to forewarn units of any impending attack, and no-man's-land must be kept clear of enemy units and installations. For this reason trench warfare is a constant round of small actions. During the summer of 1952 certain places in the line became established as the theatres of more sustained clashes in this spasmodic warfare. They were usually tactical features in the MLR or in front of it held as strongpoints by the UN forces.

Communist pressure on them slackened during the rainy season but, in September 1952, a massive barrage announced that the offensive would be renewed.

It may not have been coincidence that a US presidential election campaign was in full swing as the shells rained down on the UN front – some 45,000 of them on one September day alone. It was apparent that communist artillery strength had greatly increased as the enemy infantry emerged from behind the barrage on 6 October to attack the feature known as White Horse Hill, held by the ROK 9th Division. On the next day 93,000 rounds of artillery and mortar fire fell on the ROK troops, but supported by UN artillery and air strikes they managed to hold their positions, and were credited with destroying an entire Chinese division.

During the fight for White Horse Hill a decision was taken by the UN Command to reduce the pressure there by attacking some communist outposts near Kumwha. On 14 October two battalions of the US 7th Division and two battalions of the ROK 2nd Division began an assault on positions around Triangle Hill. Every possible artillery and air support was given but the Chinese held fast. The original objective of providing a diversion to relieve the ROK 9th Division was rapidly forgotten and the battle developed a tragic momentum of its own. Chinese reinforcements poured in to be matched by fresh UN soldiers until US 7th Infantry

Above and right: On the lookout on the MLR. Although the UN commander had decided to maintain a defensive stance, and not carry the fight far to the north, there was heavy fighting to resist communist attacks, while certain important vantage points were the scene of bloody struggles. Below: Turkish troops of the UN Command.

Division was committing a new battalion to the fighting each day. The conflict had developed into a 'prestige battle' in which the UN commanders judged it unwise to let the Chinese enjoy the sensation of preventing them achieving their objectives. The folly of this was heightened by the fact that the talks at Panmunjom – which might have been sensitive to notions of prestige – had recessed for the winter.

Eventually two weeks of costly fighting produced 8000 UN casualties and 12,000 Chinese casualties. In return for their effort the UN forces had managed to take a corner of Triangle Hill, half Sniper's Ridge and most of Jane Russell Hill. General Mark Clark's verdict on the action was that it was not a success. It was typical of the actions that took place through the summer and autumn of 1952. The 1st Marine Division fought for Bunker Hill; the US 3rd Infantry Division (which had Greek and Belgian battalions attached to it) defended the Big Nori and Kelly Hill positions; the US 2nd Infantry Division (which had a popular and dashing French battalion attached) hung on to Old Baldy and Arrowhead Hill; the US 25th Infantry Division with the fierce Turkish Brigade fought on Heartbreak Ridge; the ROK Capitol Division was in action on Finger Ridge and Capitol Hill; and the ROK 8th Division experienced stiff fighting in the Punch Bowl area.

Just like the trench warfare of World

War I, the grim little conflicts of 1952 produced disproportionate casualties for a few metres of ground gained. This was a game that the Chinese could play longer than the UN forces, and there were definite signs of war-weariness in the United States; in the election the Korean War issue helped Eisenhower and the Republicans sweep the Democrats from office. The only advantage to the UN from the fighting was that the ROK troops had emerged so well from it that they could be entrusted with two-thirds of the front line. In addition to this there was the hope of a forthcoming initiative when Eisenhower came to Korea to review the situation as president-elect. As a distinguished soldier himself he was able

to understand the harsh lesson of the 'prestige battles': that the communists would ensure that the stalemate was too costly for public opinion to endure. He also realised that the talks at Panmunjom were being used as a stalling and propaganda device to thwart the UN, but that they could become realistic and valuable if enormous military pressure was exerted on the communists. He found that most of the US generals in Korea agreed with this sombre analysis: the only way to end the struggle was through a massive offensive.

Although he had been elected president, Eisenhower would not assume office until January 1953. Until then he contented himself with some scarcely veiled threats

to the effect that the communists would not be impressed by words but by deeds 'executed under the circumstances of our own choosing' and that 'we must go ahead and do things that induce them [the communists] to want peace also'. It was high time that the deadlock was broken because the static battlefront was in danger of becoming a US Army institution. Units had become proprietorial about the ground they fought for and there was a rash of noticeboards announcing to the visitor that he entered a certain area 'by courtesy' of this or that division. The troops themselves wore flak-jackets, counted the days until rotation home, and even learned to enjoy some of the Chinese propaganda programmes boomed out

an additional reminder that US allies in the East were a force to be reckoned with, Eisenhower announced in February 1953 that the US Seventh Fleet would no longer restrain the Nationalist Chinese in Formosa from making attacks on mainland China. In fact the Seventh Fleet had not been doing much to keep the Nationalists in check for some while, but the threat implied in the US president's words caused the communist Chinese to siphon off men and materials to strengthen their garrisons on the coast opposite the island of Formosa.

Even after the failure of both Operation Strangle and then the Special Targets System, the search for ways to hurt the communist war effort through bombing was never abandoned. The last months of 1952 had seen 'concentrated' raids, in which the continuous bombing of selected river crossings was maintained for five days – the maximum period of which the UN air forces were capable. As usual the effect was disappointing: on the sixth day the communists patched up the broken bridges and started crossing once more. So, in February 1953, the UN Command switched back to the Special Targets System with another raid on the Suiho Hydro Dam. Although the communists seemed impervious to all the raids inflicted on them there is no doubt that they could have functioned much more efficiently

across the trenches from wireless loudspeakers. In return US psychological warfare units broadcast their own programmes back over the lines to the Chinese. In the middle of this apparent stability there was a constant trickle of casualties from shelling or through the activity of patrols. None of it was to the taste of General Van Fleet, who handed over command to General Maxwell Taylor in February 1953 and retired grumbling that he should have been allowed to take the offensive and force the communists from their fortifications.

Despite Van Fleet's conviction that there were enough men in Korea on the UN side to force the issue, the more usual opinion was that much greater forces would be needed and that casualties would be unacceptably high. Eisenhower was eager to see if threats alone might gain an armistice without having recourse to a major and costly offensive. Accordingly the US ambassador to India leaked the news in February that the new US Administration was prepared to resort to a nuclear attack upon China, and this was duly passed on to the Chinese. Chairman Mao had made claims that the atom bomb was a 'paper tiger', but he was not a foolish man and probably did not believe his own rhetoric. Although the Soviet Union was an atomic power it almost certainly possessed fewer systems than the United States and had no satisfactory means of delivering them to the American

mainland. The Chinese were therefore doubtful of Russian support and became doubly so when the United States exploded the first hydrogen device in November 1952.

In other ways too the Americans gave signs of preparing to expand the war. Eisenhower was prepared to allow the expansion of the ROK army by ten divisions although his predecessor had hesitated to take this step because he felt that the president of South Korea was quite powerful and independent enough with the forces already at his disposal. As

without having to combat air attacks. The cost in manpower might have been of little importance to them but the constant loss of material must have been a burden to the rudimentary economies of China and North Korea.

On 5 March Moscow Radio announced that Stalin was dead. As the senior figure in the communist world and the leader who had triumphed over the Nazi attack on Russia in 1941, Stalin had immense prestige, and had used it to persuade the Eastern communist powers to continue the Korean War, which was greatly to his advantage in drawing off NATO forces from Europe. While the Kremlin staged a power-struggle to find his successor, the Chinese were free to reassess their com-

mitment to Korea. The first sign of a thaw in their attitude came on 28 March, when they answered a request for the exchange of sick and wounded prisoners, which was duly carried out. Most significantly of all, agreement was reached that the talks at Panmunjom should be reconvened on 26 April. To go with the new talks there was what can now be seen as a further sign of hope – the communists unleashed a series of spring offensives. Although it might seem perverse, the idea behind the new attacks was to gain a better bargaining position and, because they realised this, the UN Command were as stubborn as ever in defending their ground.

The major clash in this renewal of battle

Opposite page top: President-elect Dwight D. Eisenhower visits the front line in Korea, December 1952. Opposite page bottom: Armed with a Browning automatic rifle, men of the US 179th Infantry Regiment look out over the front near Chorwon, January 1952. Below: Company K, 38th Infantry Regiment, 2nd US Infantry Division, dig in on 'Old Baldy', September 1952.

they totalled 96 men, and 20 of them were disposed in the foxholes that did duty as listening posts on the forward slope of the hill. A small US patrol had been sent forward and was moving in the valley between Pork Chop Hill and the Chinese outposts of Hasakkol when, between 2200 and 2300 hours, two companies of Chinese left Hasakkol and advanced rapidly up to the ramparts of the UN position. On their way they had a brush with the patrol and with the listening posts but they moved forward so fast that the defenders were all but overwhelmed.

In the first moments of the struggle the lieutenant commanding the small US garrison lost contact with the left-hand platoon and was cut off from his main forces in the MLR by communist shell-fire that severed the telephone line to the rear. He called for help by firing flares and obtained emergency artillery support, but, once the barrage lifted, the Chinese pressed forward and had taken most of the hill by 0200 hours. At this point a single US platoon tried to move up from the MLR to help the defenders but was driven back. At 0430 hours the Americans put in an assault by a force of five platoons and this managed to reach the position and take the high ground but was unable

occurred at the infamous Pork Chop Hill. The Chinese had at last taken Old Baldy in March (they had made heavy attacks on it the previous summer and autumn) and, from its peak, they could look down on an undistinguished hill – shaped somewhat like a pork chop – some 1300m (1420yd) to the east. About 1500m (1640yd) in front of the MLR held by the UN I Corps, 'The Chop' was not heavily garrisoned, nor was it of vital importance

to the US position, but much work had been done on its defences. A trench snaked the whole way around the perimeter of the strongpoint and this was strengthened every 30m (33yd) by stoutly constructed bunkers.

On the night of 16/17 April 1953 'The Chop' was garrisoned by two under-strength platoons from the 31st Regiment of the US 7th Infantry Division. Together with artillerymen, engineers and medics

to drive the Chinese off the hill. By this time only 55 soldiers from the three companies of Americans involved were left on the position.

While elements of both sides hung onto parts of 'The Chop' through the next day, the decision was taken by the highest level of UN Command to make every effort to regain the outpost – the Chinese were not to be allowed to claim a military ascendancy at the talks in Panmunjom. A battalion-sized attack was prepared and at 2130 hours that night the first company of US infantry stormed into the position from the south while a second company attacked unexpectedly from the north. At 0250 hours on 18 April Chinese reinforcements arrived and another US company was thrown into the growing battle. By evening the Chinese withdrew and, over the following weeks, the Americans devoted themselves to improving the defences of 'The Chop' while the Chinese artillery and mortars concentrated their fire upon it.

The struggle for Pork Chop Hill was far from over at this stage; indeed it was to escalate through June and July until the Americans had five battalions holding the feature. On 10 July the UN Command concluded that so much effort was not worthwhile and evacuated the hill a fortnight before the armistice was signed. In its way the battle for Pork Chop Hill was typical of all the major actions fought during the static period of the war. It was an unbelievably costly maul for both sides but, while ostensibly for a comparatively unimportant military objective, its real significance was as a factor in the seemingly endless armistice negotiations – a small part of larger game.

Opposite page top: The US 37th Field Artillery Battalion provides supporting fire during the battle for 'Old Baldy', October 1952. Opposite page below: Privates William Curtis and Frederick Keuch of the 9th Infantry Regiment, 2nd US Infantry Division, string barbed wire on Old Baldy, November 1952. Above: Pork Chop Hill, seen from the main line of resistance on the day it was evacuated by the US 7th Division.

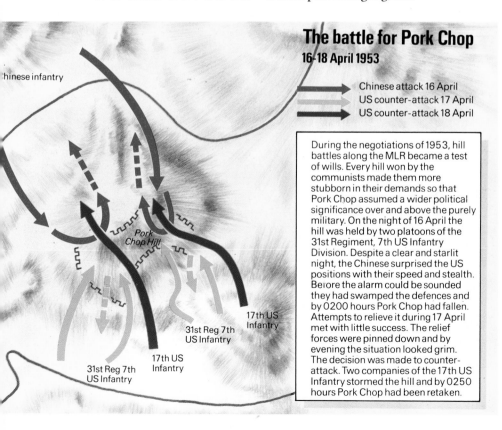

The battle for Pork Chop
16-18 April 1953

Chinese attack 16 April
US counter-attack 17 April
US counter-attack 18 April

Chinese infantry

Pork Chop Hill

17th US Infantry

31st Reg 7th US Infantry

17th US Infantry

31st Reg 7th US Infantry

During the negotiations of 1953, hill battles along the MLR became a test of wills. Every hill won by the communists made them more stubborn in their demands so that Pork Chop assumed a wider political significance over and above the purely military. On the night of 16 April the hill was held by two platoons of the 31st Regiment, 7th US Infantry Division. Despite a clear and starlit night, the Chinese surprised the US positions with their speed and stealth. Before the alarm could be sounded they had swamped the defences and by 0200 hours Pork Chop had fallen. Attempts to relieve it during 17 April met with little success. The relief forces were pinned down and by evening the situation looked grim. The decision was made to counter-attack. Two companies of the 17th US Infantry stormed the hill and by 0250 hours Pork Chop had been retaken.

10. The Air and Sea War

When the Korean People's Army (KPA) thrust across the 38th parallel into South Korea on 25 June 1950 it was supported by a small air force comprising a fighter regiment and a ground-attack regiment, backed up by a training regiment. This force had been trained and equipped by the Soviet Union. At the outbreak of hostilities it had a strength of 70 piston-engined fighters (Yak-3s, Yak-7s, Yak-9s and La-7s), around 60 Il-10 ground-attack aircraft and some 30 second-line trainers. The North Korean pilots, although for the most part young and inexperienced,

were confident and aggressive. Their confidence was certainly justified as far as South Korea's air arm was concerned; they were opposed by merely a dozen training and liaison aircraft.

The nearest United States Air Force (USAF) combat units were based in Japan, where the Fifth Air Force had the primary mission of air defence. This task was carried out by three jet-fighter wings, equipped with the Lockheed F-80C Shooting Star. They were the 8th Fighter-Bomber Wing at Itazuke, the 49th Fighter-Bomber Wing at Misawa and the 35th

Below: B-26 Invaders release their bomb loads over North Korea. The Invader was particularly useful in an interdiction role, striking at KPA communications. Above right: A P-51 Mustang releases two napalm bombs over communist targets. This aircraft was part of the 18th Fighter Bomber Wing of the Fifth Air Force. Although obsolete as an air superiority fighter by the early 1950s the reliability and range of the Mustang made it effective in a fighter-bomber role.

Fighter-Interceptor Wing at Yokota. Two All-Weather Fighter Squadrons (the 68th at Itazuke and the 359th at Yokota) flew piston-engined F-82 Twin Mustangs, and the 8th Tactical Reconnaissance Squadron was equipped with RF-80As at Yokota. The 3rd Bombardment Wing operated two squadrons of twin-engined B-26 Invaders from Johnson Air Base near Tokyo and air transport was provided by the C-54 Skymasters of the 374th Troop Carrier Wing at Tachikawa. Two other subordinate commands supplemented the Fifth Air Force. They were the Twentieth Air Force based on Okinawa, which also controlled a wing of B-29 Superfortress bombers on Guam, and the Thirteenth Air Force from the Philipines.

Evacuation and supply

The USAF's first task in South Korea was to provide cover for the merchant ships evacuating American civilians from Inchon and Seoul. Fighter patrols of F-82 Twin Mustangs operated in relays over the port of Inchon, because the F-80C jets had insufficient range for this duty when operating from their bases in Japan. On 27 June, with North Korean troops near-ing Seoul, an airlift evacuation was hastily mounted by C-54s and C-47s. The trans-port aircraft were escorted by F-82s, with F-80Cs flying top cover as their fuel consumption was not so great at high altitudes. It was the F-82s which first saw action that day, shooting down three North Korean Yak fighters which at-tempted to strafe Kimpo airfield. Later in the day the F-80Cs successfully inter-cepted a formation of eight Il-10s and shot down four of the enemy attack air-craft. These fighter actions enabled 748 refugees to be evacuated by air, while a further 905 left by sea.

In the meantime, President Harry Truman had decided to commit American air and naval forces in support of the South Koreans, a decision closely followed by a United Nations' resolution urging member nations to provide military aid for the South. The only immediate assist-ance in prospect for the hard-pressed Republic of Korea (ROK) army was the air support that could be provided by the US Far East Air Forces (FEAF).

Changes in the air

US B-29s over North Korea.

The air war in Korea differed in several respects from World War II, although similarities differed of course. Piston-engined veterans of the earlier conflict, notably the F-51 Mustang, B-26 Invader and the B-29 Superfortress, all served in Korea. Yet, apart from the Invader's interdiction operations, which were similar to those carried out in Italy in the final year of World War II, they were employed in a quite different manner.

The Mustangs were used principally for close air support in Korea, whereas in World War II they had served in bomber escort and air superiority roles. The B-29s were used principally against interdiction targets rather than strategic objectives as in World War II. Extensive jet fighter operations were the great innovation of Korea, with jet-powered F-80s and F-84s undertaking close air-support and inter-diction missions, while F-86 Sabres battled with MiG-15s for command of the air.

Unlike World War II, Korea was a limited war and all strategic and tacti-cal targets in China and the Soviet Union were off-limits to UN air attack. Nevertheless, the battle for air superiority was quickly won and a higher proportion of tactical aircraft could be allocated to close air support and interdiction targets than in World War II, when the Axis fighter force was a factor to be reckoned with until late in 1944.

In an attempt to halt the North Korean advance on the line of the Han River south of Seoul, the Fifth Air Force's fighters and bombers were ordered to attack enemy forces moving south from the 38th parallel. The F-80Cs were operating at extreme range and so carried no bombs or rockets underwing, yet their 0.5in machine guns proved to be effective against the North Korean columns which crowded the roads heading south. The B-29 Superfortresses of the Guam-based 19th Bombardment Wing had moved forward to Okinawa and they directed their 9075kg (20,000lb) bomb loads against enemy troops and their supplies. The C-54 transports of the 374th Troop Carrier Wing airlifted urgently needed ammunition to the ROK army, flying in some 200 tonnes per day until supplies began to arrive by sea.

As well as attempting to slow down the KPA's advance, the FEAF also had to deal with the enemy air force. This had made its presence felt in a series of attacks on airfields in the South. On 28 June marauding Yaks had damaged a C-54 over Suwon

and destroyed a second on the ground there, threatening to close the airfield to the USAF unless friendly fighter cover could be provided. As a result the FEAF were authorised to attack enemy airfields north of the 38th parallel.

The first attack was mounted by B-26s of the 3rd Bombardment Wing on 29 June, which knocked out some 25 enemy aircraft on the ground at Pyongyang and shot down the only North Korean fighter which attempted to intercept. Air action against North Korean airfields continued throughout July, the Fifth Air Force's attacks being supplemented by carrier strikes flown from USS *Valley Forge* and HMS *Triumph*. By the end of the month the North Korean air force had virtually ceased to exist, with UN pilots claiming more than 100 enemy aircraft destroyed on the ground or in the air.

The British naval presence was in response to the UN call for assistance. The Fleet Air Arm was to commit Seafire, Sea Fury and Firefly piston-engined naval aircraft to the war, flying from the aircraft carriers HMS *Glory*, HMS *Ocean*, HMS *Theseus* and HMS *Triumph*. Similarly, Australia provided a fighter squadron for service in Korea – No 77 Squadron RAAF, which was initially equipped with piston-engined F-51 Mustangs and later flew twin-jet Gloster Meteor fighters on air combat and ground-attack missions. South Africa assigned No 2 Squadron SAAF to the conflict, flying Mustangs and later F-86F Sabres. Although these allied air units – and also South Korean Mustang fighters – fought alongside the Americans, it was the combat squadrons of the USAF, the US Navy and US Marine Corps which bore the brunt of the air war.

Air power alone could not stem the communist advance, however, and by the end of June the Han River defences were breached and the KPA pressed on towards the strategic port of Pusan at the southeast tip of the Korean peninsula. It was at this stage that US troops were committed to the conflict and the 374th Troop Carrier Wing began to fly the US Army's 24th Infantry Division into Pusan. Clearly air support of ground forces was going to be of vital importance and the Fifth Air Force began to rectify the shortcomings in its equipment and tactics that the early operations had revealed.

Since the outward and return flights from bases in Japan consumed so much fuel, it was obviously worth considering using airfields in South Korea either as forward airfields where Japanese-based aircraft could land to refuel and rearm, or as bases in their own right. The problem was that the South Korean airfields had been built by the Japanese in World War II and, until resurfaced by US aviation engineers, were totally unsuitable for operations by jet fighters. A short-term solution was the introduction of the F-51 Mustang into the combat theatre. This piston-engined veteran of World War II had both the range and warload to operate effectively in the close air-support role. It was also capable of using the South Korean airfields, as was demonstrated by a small force of 10 F-51s which were pressed into service as close air-support aircraft at the end of June. A further 145 F-51s were withdrawn from Air National Guard units in the United States and shipped out to Korea.

By the beginning of August 1950 the ground battle for Pusan was under way and the fighter-bomber squadrons of the Fifth Air Force were heavily committed to close air support of the UN forces. Offshore the carriers of Task Force 77,

USS *Valley Forge* and USS *Philippine Sea*, mounted close air-support and interdiction missions. Even the B-29 Superfortresses were thrown into the fray. By this time four US-based B-29 units had been transferred to the Far East and so 98 of these four-engined bombers could be put into the air on 15 August for a saturation bombing raid on North Korean troop concentrations near Pusan.

The need to coordinate and control close air-support missions led to the introduction of airborne tactical coordinators, flying L-5 Sentinel liaison aircraft equipped with VHF radios. It was soon discovered that the L-5s lacked the performance necessary for this demanding and dangerous role and so the task was taken over by faster T-6 Texan trainers. Codenamed Mosquitoes, these aircraft continued for the remainder of the war to coordinate armed-reconnaissance and those battlefield-support strikes which could not be directed from the ground.

Many of the problems of close air support and interdiction were resolved by the introduction of the F-84 Thunderjet into the combat theatre in December 1950. This versatile jet fighter-bomber combined good range characteristics – 1080km (670 miles) when carrying wing-tip tanks – with a heavy armament of six

0.5in machine guns plus up to 1810kg (4000lb) of bombs or rockets. This meant that the F-84s could carry out armed reconnaissance, close air-support or interdiction missions with equal facility and they had the range, firepower and manoeuvrability to fly bomber escort missions.

The employment of B-29 bombers varied according to the tactical situation. Their use against North Korean troop concentrations was somewhat controversial and it seems probable that the mass attack on 15 August inflicted few enemy casualties. One problem in finding satisfactory targets for the bombers was the lack of strategic targets in North Korea. Most of the sources of enemy war material were in communist China or the Soviet Union, which the B-29s were prohibited from attacking.

The interdiction campaign

With China's entry into the war in October 1950, the B-29s came under attack from MiG-15 interceptors when operating over North Korea, and were forced to switch to night attacks, using radar-directed bombing techniques. As the communist night defences improved in efficiency, escorts of Marine F3D Skyknight and USAF F-94 Starfire night

fighters were provided and the B-29s began using electronic countermeasures. By the end of the war the Superfortresses had flown over 21,000 sorties and had dropped some 167,000 tonnes of bombs for the loss of 34 aircraft.

Interdiction sorties which sought to destroy enemy reinforcements and supplies before they reached the battlefront had been an important element in the FEAF's campaign to stem the North Korean advance on Pusan. Yet in early September this offensive had lost its momentum and the UN forces' breakout from Pusan, coupled with the amphibious landings at Inchon, had led to the virtual collapse of the KPA. Thereafter the advance of the UN forces was rapid and by the end of October they had occupied most of North Korea. At this juncture the Chinese communists entered the war and their massed ground assaults drove the UN forces back into South Korea. The line then stabilised south of Suwon and Wonju and the conflict degenerated into a war of attrition. Under these circumstances air interdiction came into its own.

The B-29 Superfortresses operated against targets deep in the North such as bridges, supply centres and troop concentrations. Road and rail traffic moving south, usually under cover of darkness,

Right: A US Grumman F9F Panther jet is firmly secured on board the carrier Philippine Sea. *Inset: Pre-flight briefing, discussing targets and possible enemy reaction.*

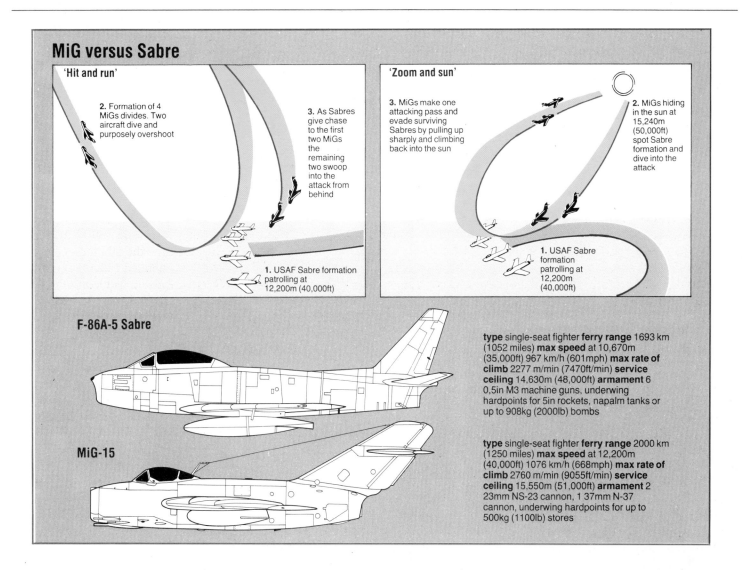

MiG versus Sabre

'Hit and run'

2. Formation of 4 MiGs divides. Two aircraft dive and purposely overshoot

3. As Sabres give chase to the first two MiGs the remaining two swoop into the attack from behind

1. USAF Sabre formation patrolling at 12,200m (40,000ft)

'Zoom and sun'

3. MiGs make one attacking pass and evade surviving Sabres by pulling up sharply and climbing back into the sun

2. MiGs hiding in the sun at 15,240m (50,000ft) spot Sabre formation and dive into the attack

1. USAF Sabre formation patrolling at 12,200m (40,000ft)

F-86A-5 Sabre

type single-seat fighter **ferry range** 1693 km (1052 miles) **max speed** at 10,670m (35,000ft) 967 km/h (601mph) **max rate of climb** 2277 m/min (7470ft/min) **service ceiling** 14,630m (48,000ft) **armament** 6 0,5in M3 machine guns, underwing hardpoints for 5in rockets, napalm tanks or up to 908kg (2000lb) bombs

MiG-15

type single-seat fighter **ferry range** 2000 km (1250 miles) **max speed** at 12,200m (40,000ft) 1076 km/h (668mph) **max rate of climb** 2760 m/min (9055ft/min) **service ceiling** 15,550m (51,000ft) **armament** 2 23mm NS-23 cannon, 1 37mm N-37 cannon, underwing hardpoints for up to 500kg (1100lb) stores

came under attack from B-26 Invaders. They had little in the way of specialised night-attack equipment, but could often use the headlights of enemy truck convoys as bomb-aiming points. Alternatively the target area could be illuminated by flares dropped from 'Lightning Bug' C-47s. The flares usually ignited at about 1675m (5500ft). Floating down beneath their parachutes, they provided four to five minutes of brilliant illumination. On the first occasion that they were used, 30 communist trucks were claimed as destroyed or damaged. Finally, the tactical fighter-bombers took their toll of enemy troops and supplies. During five days of the communist Chinese advance southwards (1–5 January 1951), Fifth Air Force fighter-bombers, flying armed reconnaissance missions behind the front line, claimed 8000 communist troops as casualties. The total number of casualties inflicted by air attack during the advance

was estimated at 40,000 troops.

Communist attempts to carry out air attacks on UN troops were limited to night-time nuisance raids by 'Bedcheck Charlies'. These were usually antiquated Polikarpov Po-2 biplanes armed with light bombs. Only occasionally were their

Above: The results of a raid by carrier-borne aircraft on the locomotive repair shed at Rashin, December 1952.

Left: US Sabres, the planes that won the battle for air superiority in Korea.
Above: The last moments of a MiG-15, captured by the nose camera of a Sabre.
Right: Close support for ground troops, provided by a Marine Corsair which can be observed wheeling away, having dropped its napalm on communist positions.

attacks more than pin-pricks, although on the night of 16/17 June 1951 two Po-2s did succeed in destroying one of the 4th Fighter-Interceptor Wing's F-86 Sabres and damaging a further eight. The slow-flying biplanes operated at low level and were difficult to intercept by radar-equipped night fighters. However, piston-engined F4U Corsair and F7F Tigercat night fighters of the US Marine Corps enjoyed some successes against them. Other types flown on night intruder missions included Yak-18 trainers and La-11 fighters.

One of the most significant results of China's entry into the war was the resurgence of communist air power. MiG-15 jet fighters operating from airfields around Antung in Manchuria, which was off-limits to US air attack, quickly established an ascendancy over the piston-engined B-29 bombers flying daylight missions in northwestern Korea. The MiG-15's bid for air superiority did not go uncontested, however. In November 1950 the F-86A Sabres of the USAF's 4th Fighter-Interceptor Wing (FIW) left the United States for Japan aboard the aircraft carrier USS *Cape Esperance*. By mid-December the

first F-86As were operating from Kimpo in South Korea and on 17 December Lieutenant-Colonel Bruce Hinton scored the first of nearly 800 victories over MiG-15s which were to be claimed by Sabres during the war.

The Sabre's combat record in Korea was by any standards impressive. Of the 900 aerial victories claimed by USAF pilots during the war, 792 were MiG-15s shot down by Sabres. The MiGs in their turn managed to knock down only 78 Sabres. American fighter pilots thus established a ten-to-one kill/loss ratio in their favour. This result was by no means easily won, as the Sabres were handicapped in several ways when compared to their opponents.

When operating over northwestern Korea, in an area soon to be christened 'MiG Alley', the Sabres were limited in their endurance. An F-86A with full internal fuel and two 545-litre (120-gallon) drop tanks was restricted to some 20 minutes over the Yalu River, whereas the MiG-15s were within a few minutes' flying time of their bases in Manchuria. This situation worsened in January 1951 when the Chinese advance forced the 4th FIW's

Above: Captain Joseph McConnell, the leading US ace in Korea with 16 kills, all MiG-15s.

Sabres to evacuate Kimpo and withdraw to Japan. The Chinese air force did not fully exploit this temporary advantage, however, and by the end of the month the situation on the ground had stabilised sufficiently for the South Korean airfields to be put back into operation. Thereafter, the F-86s continued to operate from Suwon and Kimpo. Early in 1952 a second Sabre wing, the 51st FIW, commanded by the World War II ace Francis Gabreski, joined the air battles over the Yalu River.

MiG versus Sabre

Apart from the Sabre's range problems, it was also inferior to the MiG-15 in various aspects of performance, although on balance the F-86 was generally considered to be the better aircraft. The MiG could outclimb the Sabre at all altitudes, whereas the latter was marginally faster in level flight. The MiG-15's greater operational ceiling gave it an initial advantage in combat, yet although it had a greater initial acceleration in a dive, the heavier Sabre had the advantage in a sustained dive. The MiG's zoom climb and tight turning characteristics (except

at high speeds) were valuable, but the fighter's good points were counterbalanced by such undesirable features as poor control at high speeds, a low rate of roll and directional instability at high altitudes. Its heavy armament (two 23mm and one 37mm cannon) was better suited to bomber interception than to fighter-versus-fighter combat; but the Sabre's six 0.5in machine guns, while having a faster rate of fire, lacked the range and hitting power necessary for jet combat.

Sabres operating in 'MiG Alley' faced large formations of 50 to 70 enemy fighters flying at heights of 15,250m (50,000ft) or more which the American fighters could not match. This meant that the US fighter pilots had to evolve tactics to cope with a 'bounce' by fast-flying MiGs diving down on them from high altitude at a time and place of the enemy's choosing. The solution was the 'jet stream' of 16 Sabres divided into four-aircraft flights, each of which entered 'MiG Alley' at five-minute intervals and at different altitudes between 8200 and 10,050m (27,000 and 33,000ft). The Sabres flew at high speed (typically Mach 0.87) so that as soon as one flight was engaged by

the MiGs, the others could rapidly converge on the combat. The flights adopted a 'fluid four' tactical formation, comprising two element leaders each covered by a wingman. So, although operating at a considerable initial disadvantage against the high-flying MiGs, the mutually supporting Sabre formations were able to meet the MiGs' 'bounce' with a vigorous counter-attack.

If jet-versus-jet fighter combat was the most dramatic innovation of the Korean air war, then the combat service of the helicopter in Korea was equally significant. Casualty evacuation was undertaken by Sikorsky H-5s, Bell OH-13s and Hiller H-23s, the wounded being carried in panniers attached to the sides of the helicopter fuselage. This enabled wounded troops to receive speedy medical attention at field hospitals and so reduced fatalities. USAF H-5 and Sikorsky H-19 helicopters were used for combat rescue missions, including the recovery of airmen shot down behind communist lines. US Navy Sikorsky HO3S helicopters operating from carriers carried out similar missions. Army and Marine Corps helicopters operated as airborne command

Left: In Korea the helicopter was in its infancy, but proved valuable for the evacuation of wounded. Below: The USS New Jersey *provides a formidable weight of shell fire as she fires all nine of her 16-in guns onto communist positions – a role she was also to play three decades later in the Lebanon. Right: Task Force 77 moves into Korean waters, May 1953. The photograph has been taken from the battleship USS Missouri.*

posts and on observation duties, and H-19 transport helicopters were used for troop and cargo transport.

When the Korean War ended on 27 July 1953 the air units of the USAF, US Navy, US Marine Corps and allied air forces had flown 1,040,708 sorties. They had succeeded in mastering the enemy air forces to such an extent that the UN ground forces had seldom come under air attack. Conversely, communist troops were harassed night and day by allied air attacks ranging in scope from massed raids by B-29 bombers to strafing runs by fighter-bombers. Tactical air power was therefore a key weapon in the Korean conflict, because it enabled the UN forces successfully to counter massed attacks by vastly more numerous communist ground forces.

The sea war in Korea

Unlike the air war in Korea, the sea war was often an undramatic, unpublicised effort. But the Korean War could not have been sustained by the UN without naval power, as six out of seven UN personnel who fought in Korea went there by sea. Essentially it was sea power which kept the UN Command supplied and in action throughout the war.

The sea war showed the complete interdependence of all three services involved. Korea is a peninsula, and the UN navies (of which of course the US Navy was the most important and largest

component) controlled Korean waters up to the Soviet and Chinese borders. This situation had a number of military advantages, giving scope for amphibious landings, coastal bombardment, blockade, and air interdiction operations from carriers. In a more general context, the UN navies played a very significant part in offsetting the advantages enjoyed by communist manpower resources in the region. The Chinese might have been able to mass their forces in what Mac-Arthur called the 'privileged sanctuary' of Manchuria but once they had entered the Korean peninsula they were often at the mercy of opposing forces deployed

by the UN navies in one form or another.

President Truman had decreed a naval blockade on 30 June 1950. But during the first six months of the Korean War, the primary naval emphasis was on amphibious operations. There were landings at Pohang, Inchon, Wonsan, and when the time came in December 1950, following the Chinese incursion into Korea, X Corps was successfully evacuated from northeast Korea by the UN navies. These operations were a classic illustration of the flexibility of sea power in an extremely difficult political and military situation.

During the summer and autumn of 1951, before the land fighting congealed

along the Main Line of Resistance (MLR) in November of that year, some thought was given by the UN Command planners to another amphibious landing at Kojo, about 50km (31 miles) south of Wonsan on Korea's east coast. The planners envisaged a MacArthurian thrust into the rear of the communist armies on the eastern front. But when General Omar Bradley, the chairman of the US Joint Chiefs of Staff (JCS) visited the Far East in October 1951, he cancelled the operation, stating that no more of the enemy's 'real estate' was needed.

As amphibious operations were ruled out by high policy, the primary naval

emphasis during the two years of the so-called 'stalemate' war of 1951–3 was on blockade and carrier air interdiction operations. Other sea operations included minesweeping, escort work, and anti-submarine patrols. There was a logical connection between blockade and interdiction as the blockade forced the communists to concentrate their resupply efforts to North Korea on that country's overstretched road and rail network. Interdiction and naval bombardment of coastal railways then took up the task of further eroding the communist supply system.

When the blockade was established at

the beginning of the war, limits had been set up to keep the UN navies away from the sensitive Russian and Chinese borders. In the Sea of Japan, the blockade line ended north of Chongjin to keep UN ships away from the Vladivostok complex. In the Yellow Sea, the blockade excluded the mouth of the Yalu River where the Sino-Korean borders met. But south of these areas there was a systematic blockade operation against North Korea's coastline.

The blockade force had been created in the first days of the war from ships of the US and Royal Navies in the Far East. On 12 September 1950 the Blockade Force

Right: Three ships of the US Navy off Korea: the USS Buck, *the USS* St Paul, *and the USS* Wisconsin. *Below: Even after the signing of the ceasefire, the US Navy still had a role to play. Here, Indian troops are about to board a US carrier to be flown by helicopter to the neutral buffer zone, September 1953.*

was designated Task Force 95, 'UN Blockading and Escort Force'. TF 95 was then divided into two, with Task Group 95.1 on station on the Korean west coast, while TG 95.2 was responsible for the east coast. TG 95.1 was under the command of a British rear-admiral for most of the war, and two RN light carriers, *Triumph* and *Ocean,* were to play a major part in these operations in the Yellow Sea.

Overall command arrangements for the Blockade Force which were to last for the duration were formalised early in 1951. Task Force 95 was placed under the commander of the US Seventh Fleet, who then delegated his operational control to the senior cruiser commander of TF 77, the fast carrier group which operated throughout the war in the Sea of Japan with four big flattops of the US Navy. TF 95 came under the command of the Seventh Fleet according to these arrangements on 3 April 1951. This made for flexibility as army and air force units could ask for naval support simply by contacting the commander of the Seventh Fleet. The line of command then extended upwards from the Seventh Fleet to the

US Commander Naval Forces Far East in Tokyo. Vice-Admiral C. Turner Joy held this post from the outbreak of war to 4 June 1952, when he was succeeded by Vice-Admiral R. P. Briscoe, who then served for the remainder of the Korean War.

The operations of the two blockade groups reflected the differing conditions in the Yellow Sea and the Sea of Japan. In the more restricted area off the Korean west coast, there was a light carrier element and a surface element of frigates and minesweepers. In the Sea of Japan, TG 95.2 was divided into four separate elements to patrol the very long coastline from the front to north of Chongjin.

It was soon discovered that the main North Korean supply route from Vladivostok to Wonsan was vulnerable to naval bombardment between Songjin and Hungnam. The blockade force in the Sea of Japan included some of the biggest ships afloat, and altogether four US Navy battleships were used in the programme of coastal bombardment: *Missouri, Iowa, New Jersey* and *Wisconsin.* These battleships were also often called to give close support to the UN ground forces at the

eastern end of the MLR. Their 16in guns had a range of 32km (20 miles) and this punch was much feared by the communists, according to the testimony of prisoners-of-war.

Blockade and bombardment were only part of the naval effort during 1951–3, however. The aircraft from TF 77, on station in the Sea of Japan, played an important part in the continuing interdiction campaign against the North Korean transportation system.

It was agreed with the USAF that TF 77 would work on the Chinese and North Korean supply routes east of Longitude 127. During 1952 most of the air-strike potential of TF 77 was employed in Operation Strangle, the joint interdiction effort. The carriers of the Blockade Force, TF 95, were also used in this campaign, and it was estimated that about 70% of their air potential was used during this period against the communist supply routes. The interdiction programme was only partially successful, however, and by 1953 Operation Strangle was phased out. But interdiction had played a significant role in eroding communist pressure on the MLR.

Two other aspects of the sea war in Korea contributed significantly to the war of attrition waged by the UN Command against the communist forces. The first of these was the prolonged naval operation in which the North Korean east coast ports of Wonsan, Hungnam and Songjin were 'besieged' from 1951 to the very day of the armistice on 27 July 1953. Not only were these ports denied to communist shipping, but this effort by the UN tied down large numbers of North Korean troops and much heavy equipment.

Wonsan, for example, was the most important port in North Korea. But a cluster of islands in the outer harbour was occupied continuously from early 1951 onwards, so denying use of the port to the communists. On Yo-do Island 6km (4 miles) from Wonsan, a base was set up with an airstrip and garrisoned at differing periods by US, British, and South Korean Marines. US naval historians have noted that the American naval commander of the special task element which resupplied these islands

was awarded the title of 'Mayor of Wonsan' courtesy of the US Navy, but that it was 'a non-political title'.

Another little-publicised naval operation was the occupation of strategic offshore North Korean islands by South Korean Marines, backed by vessels of TF 95, the Blockade Force. These islands included Nan-do off the North Korean east coast near Kojo, and the Yang-do group near Songjin. There was a similar operation in the Yellow Sea where Cho-do and Sok-to in the Taedong estuary were held for most of the period from 1951 to 1953. The UN navies also made sure that Paengnyong-do and four other associated islands off the North Korean coast were occupied for the duration. This particular island group lay south of the 38th parallel near the Ongjin peninsula and custody was retained by the UN Commander-in-Chief by the armistice of July 1953.

The occupation of these offshore islands, which was classified information at the time, gave several important military

advantages to the UN Command. They were used as radar, radio, and electronic intelligence stations, as well as air-sea rescue bases. From these islands were launched special operations against the North Korean mainland. From here agents were systematically infiltrated into communist territory. The radio and electronic listening posts installed on these islands played an important part in the air war against North Korea. But it was the UN navies which supplied and maintained these island outposts. With the armistice of July 1953, the islands were abandoned – but not before they had been used for evacuating thousands of anti-communist guerrillas who had been operating behind the communist lines in North Korea.

In all these ways, the UN navies in Korea played an indispensable part in eroding the communist military effort for relatively little cost to the UN forces. Control of the seas around Korea was one of the cornerstones of the UN effort in the Korean War.

11. The Elusive Peace

On 4 December 1950, with the Chinese offensive rapidly gaining ground, Truman and Attlee met in Washington following the president's incautious remarks at a press conference implying that atomic weapons might be used against the Chinese. It was tacitly agreed to abandon the policy of reunification and to settle for a ceasefire along the 38th parallel. Ironically, at the very moment that the West's resolve weakened, the Chinese were privately indicating a willingness to negotiate, despite their public rejection of mediation by 13 Asian and Arab states. The Americans were, however, suspicious of Chinese intentions, and the moment was lost. By the late spring of 1951, with the military situation reversed in the UN's favour, the Americans made new attempts to open negotiations. In May George Kennan, a former State Department official well known to the Soviet Union and on leave of absence at Princeton, was asked to contact the Soviet ambassador to the UN, Jacob Malik. As a result of their meetings, Malik unexpectedly broadcast on the UN's weekly radio programme on 23 June announcing Soviet interest in peace talks. Chinese newspapers approved the proposal and on 29 June the UN Commander-in-Chief, General Ridgway, broadcast his own invitation to enemy commanders to meet him on the Danish hospital ship, *Jutlandia*. Radio Peking replied in kind on 2 July suggesting Kaesong as the site for a meeting. Liaison officers met there on 8 July and the first formal session of armistice negotiations began on 10 July 1951. It was expected that it might take three to six weeks to conclude an agreement. In fact, it was to take another two years and 17 days and another 14,000 UN casualties before the talks were resolved.

Both sides approached the negotiations with different intentions. The Joint Chiefs of Staff (JCS) had instructed Ridgway to arrange an armistice without discussing any final settlement of the war or any issues other than purely military questions. There was also concern to establish an armistice line not on the 38th parallel but along the more naturally defensible 'Kansas Line' which ran approximately 16km (10 miles) to the north of the parallel. By contrast the North Korean and Chinese delegates were interested only in the 38th parallel as a demarcation line.

The talks began in the spirit in which they were to continue. Thus the communists objected to the seats the UN Command liaison officers had arbitrarily chosen to occupy at the initial meeting on

8 July. It was later appreciated that as these seats faced south it implied, to the oriental mind, that the occupants were the conquerors. Thereafter, whenever the delegations met, the communists were careful to occupy the south-facing seats before the UN team arrived. The chief UN Command delegate, Vice-Admiral C. Turner Joy, also discovered that he had been given a ridiculously low chair, enabling his communist counterpart, Colonel-General Nam Il, to tower over him across the table. Discussions at Kaesong were frequently acrimonious and the communists staged a number of 'incidents' in the neutral zone around the conference centre, such as an accusation on 19 August that a 'security patrol' had been ambushed by UN forces. On 22 August they claimed that the UN Command had bombed Kaesong in an attempt to murder the communist delegation. At other times the UN and communist delegations faced each other in complete silence for periods of up to two hours.

The first dispute concerned precisely what would be discussed and it took

until 26 July to agree an agenda since the communists persisted in demanding that it include a specific reference to the 38th parallel. As eventually adopted, the agenda listed five main issues for negotiation: first, that an agenda be adopted; secondly, that a military demarcation line be estab- lished together with a demilitarised zone as a pre-condition for the cessation of hostilities; thirdly, that arrangements be made for a ceasefire and armistice with agreement on a suitable supervisory organisation to carry out the arrangements; fourthly, that agreement be reached on

Opposite page: The wintry landscape of Korea is suddenly illuminated by the firing of US artillery. Above: Mark Clark and his staff watch an exchange of prisoners at Panmunjom, May 1953. Left: While the talking went on, so did the killing and the dying. Here, a US infantryman comes under heavy artillery fire during an advance into communist positions.

the exchange of prisoners-of-war; and, lastly, that appropriate recommendations be made to the governments concerned on a post-armistice settlement. Having agreed the agenda, the delegations proceeded to discuss the demarcation line, but the bombing 'incident' led to the talks being broken off on 23 August. Ridgway was now determined to move the talks away from communist-dominated Kaesong. While liaison officers considered a solution, Van Fleet was authorised to launch a limited offensive to inflict maximum casualties on the Chinese and to secure as much commanding ground as possible. The offensive appears to have persuaded the communists to come back to the talks on 25 October at the newly agreed site of Panmunjom.

Negotiations resumed on a demarcation line and on 23 November it was agreed that it should be the actual line of contact between the opposing armies from which both sides would withdraw 2km (1½ miles). A sub-committee would determine the line and this would become the demarcation line provided an armistice was signed within 30 days. Ratified on 27 November 1951, the agreement held out the hope that the war would end soon, but in its eagerness to achieve a ceasefire the UN Command had presented the communists with a 30-day de facto ceasefire and had halted the military pressure Van Fleet had been applying. The 30-day period passed without further agreement while the communists reinforced their front line and built formidable new defences. Ridgway was particularly incensed by this premature concession, the suspension of the offensive having removed any incentive the communists might have had to reach an agreement. Admiral Joy was later to comment that 'in debating with the Communists there is no substitute for the imperative logic of military pressure ...'.

Negotiations during the 30-day period had centred on the third item on the agenda. The principle of creating a Military Armistice Commission (MAC) and Neutral Nations Supervisory Commission (NNSC) was quickly agreed but there was dispute over the acceptability of the communist nomination of the

Soviet Union as a 'neutral'. There was also discussion on inspection of each side by teams from the NNSC, the construction of new airfields after the armistice, and the means by which 'foreign' troops should be rotated without increasing overall numbers. The NNSC members eventually agreed on were Sweden and Switzerland (nominated by UN Command) and Poland and Czechoslovakia (nominated by the communists). Although some issues under this agenda item remained to be resolved, it was settled for all practical purposes by May 1952. Agreement on the last agenda item had been achieved earlier with both sides accepting on 19 February 1952 that a political conference should be held within three months of the armistice signing to provide a final settlement.

There remained only one issue of substance – the exchange of prisoners – but this was to prove the most intractable problem of all and to delay the final agreement for another year. The matter was first raised on 11 December 1951 and the two sides exchanged lists of prisoners-of-war seven days later. The UN Command list contained 132,000 names of Chinese or North Korean prisoners but the communist list contained only 11,559 names, while they had claimed in March 1951 to be holding 65,000 prisoners. Even by their own figures this implied a discrepancy of over

53,000, and there were at least 8000 missing Americans who could not be accounted for. The communists claimed that Republic of Korea (ROK) army prisoners had been allowed home, while foreigners had been 'released at the front', had been killed in UN air raids, had escaped or died. A further problem for the United Nations was that some 38,000

The conditions for prisoners on both sides were far from ideal, and prisoners played an important role as a bargaining counter during the ceasefire negotiations. Left: Communist prisoners in a camp in South Korea – the man on the right is having his head shaved to combat lice. Left centre: North Koreans in a southern camp are led away after rioting. Left bottom: US prisoners in the North take part in a propaganda parade. Right: Colonel James C. Murray for the UN and Colonel Chang Chun San for North Korea initial maps showing the demarcation zones between North and South, July 1953.

of the prisoners in UN Command hands were South Koreans, the North having extended its mobilisation orders to the South in July 1950 and simply impressed them into the Korean People's Army (KPA). It had also become apparent that many North Korean and Chinese prisoners did not wish to be repatriated. Mindful of the fate of those unwillingly repatriated to the Soviet Union at the end of World War II, the UN Command chose to make a stand on the principle of voluntary repatriation even though every delay put UN prisoners at risk.

On 2 April 1951 the communists suggested preparing new lists of those prisoners willing to accept repatriation and much to the surprise of both delegations UN Command screening revealed that only 70,000 prisoners in UN hands wished to return to the North. The communists bitterly rejected the implications and on 7 May the UN Command prison compounds on Koje Island off Pusan were the scene of planned disturbances in which the US commandant was seized. It later became apparent that communist agents had deliberately got themselves taken prisoner to organise the camps; the commandant was only released after an admission was signed that violence had been used during the screening process. The communists also attempted to divert attention from the unwillingness of their soldiers to return home by extracting false confessions from UN prisoners, principally US pilots, that they had indulged in bacteriological warfare against North Korea. With no agreement being reached at Panmunjom over voluntary repatriation, Major-General W. K. Harrison, who had succeeded Joy as chief negotiator, recessed the talks on 8 October 1952.

The deadlock was only broken by events elsewhere. In the United States the presidential election in November gave the Republican candidate, General Dwight D. Eisenhower, the largest vote ever recorded, and ended 20 years of Democratic power. Eisenhower had pledged to review the situation and end the war, a view given added emphasis by a pre-inaugural visit to Korea. In his first 'State of the Union' speech on 2 February 1953 Eisenhower announced that the Seventh Fleet would be withdrawn from Formosan waters, thereby implying that Chiang Kai-shek, the Chinese Nationalist leader, would no longer be restrained from attacking mainland China. In January American scientists had tested a new nuclear artillery shell and the JCS were now prepared to envisage a slow but ever-increasing escalation of the war should the armistice talks not be resumed. On 22 May while on a trip to Delhi, the hawkish Secretary of State, John Foster Dulles, again raised the possibility of the employment of nuclear weapons against the Chinese in unmistakable terms. In the meantime the communist world had been thrown into disarray by the death of Stalin in March 1953. This and the new US resolve resulted in immediate signs that the communists were interested in reopening negotiations and they agreed to a suggestion to exchange sick and wounded prisoners. This operation, 'Little

Above: General Mark Clark at the signing of the armistice agreement, July 1953.
Above right: Some of the fiercest fighting of the war took place in the weeks immediately preceding the signing of the armistice, as the communists strove to improve their position, and the UN forces tried to hold on to a line that would give South Korea a defensible frontier.
Below: Troops move up to 'Old Baldy', the position overlooking Pork Chop Hill.

Switch', took place between 20 April and 3 May involving the transfer of 6670 communist personnel and 684 UN Command personnel. On 26 April 1953 talks were resumed at Panmunjom.

The resumption of negotiations was not destined to bring immediate peace as the communists began a series of limited offensives. Symbolic of the continuing futility of the fighting was the battle for Pork Chop Hill, a UN outpost of the Main Line of Resistance (MLR),

and also the communist attack on the position known as 'the Hook' held by British forces during May 1953.

Syngman Rhee's intransigence

With agreement near at Panmunjom, the success of the negotiations was challenged by the South Korean president, Syngman Rhee, who was opposed to any truce that would leave Korea divided. As early as 24 April he had threatened to remove his army from the UN Command and from 25 May he boycotted the talks. He further contrived to imperil negotiations by releasing some 25,000 anti-cómmunist prisoners-of-war on 18 June, thus weakening the UN's bargaining position as far as prisoner exchange was concerned. Rhee's intransigence also appears to have motivated the biggest communist offensive for two years, a nine-day battle pushing back the South Korean II Corps an average of 5km (3 miles) along a 13km (8-mile) front between 10 and 18 June. The offensive was resumed on 13 July against both the ROK II Corps and the US IX Corps. Nine UN Command divisions were required to blunt an assault in which it was estimated that the communists fired off all the shells

accumulated during the months of stale-mate. In June and July the UN Command suffered over 14,000 casualties. On 11 July Rhee agreed to accept the armistice terms although he would not actually sign it. In return he secured from the Americans $24 billion worth of aid, an army of 20 divisions and a mutual security pact which was signed in October 1953.

The long-awaited armistice was finally signed at 10am on 27 July 1953. A military demarcation line was established which gave the North Koreans some 2200km² (850 sq. miles) south of the 38th parallel and the South some 6100km² (2350 sq. miles) north of it. A Demilitarised Zone was established, to be overseen by an MAC consisting of five nominees of each side and assisted by ten joint observer teams. The NNSC, again assisted by inspection teams, was to supervise troop rotation. Each side would have 60 days to return those prisoners-of-war who wished to be repatriated, the remaining prisoners being handed over to a Neutral Nations Repatriation Commission (NNRC) drawn from the same four members of the NNSC plus India, which would provide a custodial force for the operation. Each side then had 96 days in which to

try to persuade its nationals to return home, after which they would be dis-charged as civilians to go where they pleased. This part of the agreement – 'Big Switch' – took place between 5 August and 6 September 1953. Some 75,823 prisoners were returned to the communists and 12,773 to the UN Command, while the UN Command delivered 22,604 prisoners to the NNRC and the communists returned some 359 to the NNRC. Of these only 137 com-munist personnel chose to return to the North while 349 UN Command per-sonnel wished to remain there.

Continuing confrontation

Other parts of the armistice agreement were never finalised. The North Koreans refused to allow NNSC teams to inspect the five ports of entry stipulated and the UN Command similarly suspended in-spection as a result in May 1956. In the absence of any evidence that North Korea intended to abide by the provisions preventing future military expansion, the UN Command suspended its adherence to the same provisions in June 1957, allowing the modernisation of the ROK army to match their communist rivals.

The conference to produce a final settle-ment, which was intended to begin in October 1953, was not convened until April 1954 at Geneva. By that time there was more concern to reach agreement on the problems of Indochina and no agree-ment was concluded on Korea. The UN Commission for the Unification and Rehabilitation of Korea was finally sus-pended in 1977. The UN Command in Korea still, however, exists. The 16 states that had committed troops to Korea signed a declaration in July 1953 to carry out the armistice terms. Some maintained their military contingents in South Korea for some years, the Thais being the last to leave, in June 1972; US forces still remain. A number of the 16, such as the United Kingdom, still supply a token guard of honour to the UN Command in the MAC. Periodically the friends of North Korea, neither Korea yet being a member of the UN, attempt to dissolve the UN Command, but its mechanism remains in being. The MAC still meets regularly at Panmunjom to discuss the constant violations of the ceasefire. There has never been a formal peace treaty. Thus an armistice designed to last 90 days has endured for over 30 years.

Conclusion and Aftermath

The outcome of the Korean War continues to affect world politics in a number of ways, especially in the Far East. The original United Nations action had been authorised by the UN Security Council resolution of 27 June 1950. This recommended that 'members furnish such armed assistance to the Republic of Korea as may be necessary to repel the armed attack and to restore international peace and security in the area'.

At heavy cost, which included around 142,000 US casualties (of which some 33,000 were killed), these objectives were secured. It had proved quite impractical to unite Korea under UN auspices, as had been authorised by the UN General Assembly in October 1950. But the saving of South Korea presented the United States and its allies with a number of political and strategic benefits. There were some important military lessons to be drawn from the war, not all of them favourable to the West.

At the end of the war, however, South Korea was presented with very strong northern fortifications south of the Military Demarcation Line (MDL) and the 4km (2½-mile) Demilitarised Zone (DMZ) created by the Korean armistice of July 1953. Unlike the 38th parallel, these defences were based on terrain and water barriers. A mutual defence treaty signed between the United States and South Korea in October 1953 remains in force 'indefinitely'. US troops and air units have remained in South Korea, so providing an indispensable security guarantee, although a small UN Command still polices the armistice.

Indeed, it was on the strategic thinking

of the US defence establishment that the war had the most obvious impact. For soon after the end of hostilities in Korea, the Eisenhower administration developed the concept of massive retaliation a policy implying the use of nuclear weapons, against communist aggression, to deter another such war in future. In addition, Korea provided US analysts of the late 1950s and early 1960s, who developed the theories of 'limited war' with the most important of their examples of how an international confrontation could be kept below the nuclear threshold. The crucial episodes in the debate between MacArthur and Truman, and the discussions surrounding the decision not to use atomic weapons are all part of the small body of information that those who shape the strategic thought of the West have to use when examining the problems and possibilities facing Western statesmen.

Above, opposite page top and opposite page centre: Keeping an eye on the movements of men and material on the communist side, these observers in South Korea are part of the security apparatus that the Southern government hopes will make another invasion unlikely. Opposite page bottom: The dividing line itself; the two triangular markings are helicopter landing strips.

Military lessons

But at all levels during the Korean War, important lessons emerged which have continuing relevance. In particular, these lessons involve the relationship between military technology and manpower, and highlight the difficulties encountered by Western democratic societies in waging limited warfare.

The initial Chinese communist successes in Korea during the winter of 1950/51 were won by massed forces inadequately equipped by Western standards. These Chinese forces succeeded in sweeping the UN Command out of North Korea and in advancing south to about the 37th parallel, the Osan–Samchok line, by January 1951. But the later phases of the fluid fighting in Korea (February–July 1951) saw the UN forces, deploying heavy firepower and with considerable air support, drive the Chinese and North Koreans back above the 38th parallel. On the Soyang River on the eastern front during May 1951 the Chinese armies broke. But good political and logistic reasons led the UN Command to restrict the advance north to the defensible Main Line of Resistance (MLR).

Successful as was the 'Meatgrinder' technique in neutralising the Chinese armies, it was still an expensive business for the UN Command. Later experience in Vietnam showed that US firepower and air power could not be decisive against a well-led communist guerrilla army. But Korea was a peninsula and geography favoured the UN defenders of South Korea. Thus UN firepower, in Korean conditions, checkmated massed Chinese armies and negated Mao Tsetung's dictum that 'man not weapons' provides the decisive element in modern warfare. The subsequent debate within the Chinese military establishment between the Maoists and the supporters of modern military techniques has never been satisfactorily resolved.

Closely related to the dominance of firepower over manpower in Korea was the somewhat ambivalent lesson to be drawn from the use of air power by the UN Command in Korea. During the communist offensives of 1950–51 the UN air forces played a central role in halting the communist armies. But during the stalemate conditions of 1951–2 a massive UN air interdiction programme, Operation Strangle, was unable to prevent a continuing Chinese military build-up north of the MLR. This was due to the mass mobilisation of North Korean and Chinese labour which enabled damaged roads and railways in North Korea to be quickly repaired. This situation is analogous to that in Indochina, but only partly, because once communist offensive operations were in progress on the open Korean terrain, the UN air forces were able to operate with deadly effectiveness. The lesson remains that in combat with Asian armies, Western firepower cannot always bring quick, decisive results.

Closely related to these military lessons was the factor of political willpower. During the Korean stalemate war of 1951–3, the US and its allies faced a test of their staying power. They passed the test and it was the communists who eventually conceded the principle of

voluntary prisoner repatriation at Panmunjom. The subsequent experience of Vietnam, however, illustrates the difficulty of maintaining a protracted and unpopular Western war effort against regional communist expansion. Seen in this perspective, the Korean War may come to be viewed as a unique commitment by the United States and its allies.

Political effects

The political aftermath of the Korean War also changed the global balance of power in a number of ways. By the late autumn of 1950 the North Korean regime of Kim Il Sung had been effectively eliminated as UN armies advanced to the Yalu River. Communist China's intervention (and the subsequent expulsion of the UN forces from North Korea) restored the Pyongyang regime, albeit as a client government of Peking for the rest of the war. The Korean People's Army (KPA) never fought above corps level after Inchon.

But China's intervention in Korea and its initial victories over MacArthur's forces also made the new China a world power. Even after the UN counter-offensive in the spring and summer of 1951, China was able to hold the UN allies to a stalemate war for two years. This establishment of China's power was symbolised by the fact that the United States, as chief representative of the United Nations in Korea, was forced to give at least *de facto* recognition to Peking by negotiating with Chinese representatives for over two years. The division of Korea by the July 1953 armistice thus represented a balance of power between China and the United States in Korea.

The assertion of the Peking regime in Korea's affairs (which echoed the history of past centuries) had effects that were not clear in 1953. But by its resistance in Korea, China was to become a formidable counterweight to Moscow within the world communist movement. China now sought its own voice in world affairs; the death of Stalin in the closing months of the Korean War made Mao Tse-tung the political equal of any subsequent Soviet leader. Moreover, Chinese interests in Korea were more immediate and more involved with its national security than those of Moscow. By the end of the 1950s a whole range of issues, such as Marxist doctrine and China's demand for Soviet nuclear weapons, had come to divide Peking from Moscow. The Korean War thus began a reassessment of communist China's interests that within a decade of the 1953 Korean armistice had led to the Sino-Soviet schism.

If the Korean War brought the crystallisation of communist China as a major power, the conflict also produced great political advantages for the West. The increased level of North Atlantic rearmament made possible by the war in Korea probably deterred similar adventures by the communist bloc for the rest of the 1950s. In this way, the drift to general war was checked and the West found itself in a position where it could contain the communist powers. For their part, the Soviet and Chinese leaders seem to have realised that in the aftermath of the Korean War the world balance of forces favoured the West.

The programme of North Atlantic rearmament that underlay these developments was particularly noticeable in the case of the United States. As a result of the Korean War, annual defence appropriations rose from under $15 billion in 1950 to over $50 billion by 1953. There was a rapid expansion of conventional, mobile, naval and air forces, combined with a systematic extension of the USAF's Strategic Air Command's overseas base structure. The construction of a nuclear carrier fleet was begun, and four extra US Army divisions were sent to West Germany. A US ammunition production base was established which was not dismantled after the 1953 armistice.

This rearmament effort was financed by a significant expansion of the US economy during the Korean War. Defence expenditure rose by over $30 billion annually between 1950 and 1953, but the Gross National Product (GNP) increased by $60 billion during this period. Manufacturing capacity, meanwhile, rose by 25% from 1950 to 1953.

Of great importance was the expansion of the US nuclear arsenal, which was made politically possible by the challenge of the Korean War. When the war started in 1950, the US probably possessed under 400 atomic weapons. By 1953, the figure was probably about 1000; it seems doubtful that the Soviet Union possessed more than 100–200 by this time. Moreover, in delivery systems, with the jet B-47 bomber already in production, the US had a decisive lead. There was no equivalent Soviet bomber.

In addition to the US atomic weapons programme, the drive for the 'super', the thermonuclear bomb, was given an immense boost by the Korean War. In what was in effect a crash programme the first thermonuclear reaction was achieved in the 'Greenhouse' test of May 1951; in November 1952 a primitive thermonuclear device was exploded at Eniwetok in the Pacific. In this way, the foundations were laid for US nuclear ascendancy over the Soviet Union that was to last for 20 years.

Perhaps just as significant as these military measures expedited by the Korean War was the consolidation of the Western alliance system to include the

former enemy states of West Germany and Japan. In an agreement with the United States, Britain and France in May 1952, West Germany recovered its virtual independence, although formal sovereignty was not achieved until 1955. Perhaps even more remarkable was the agreement by the three allies for the necessity for some form of German rearmament within a North Atlantic framework. It was solely the Korean War which made this development possible.

In the Pacific, the Japanese peace treaty with the United States of September 1951, concluded with great urgency as a result of the Korean aggression, was the keystone of a new US-sponsored security system in the region. Including the Western allies, nearly 50 countries signed the treaty, but the Soviet Union refused to join. At the same time a parallel US–Japanese security treaty was signed which legitimised the US military presence in Japan. Almost simultaneously, the United States concluded security treaties with the Philippines and with Australia and New Zealand, the ANZUS Pact. The Pacific security system which was thus created in 1951 as a direct result of the Korean War has lasted with surprisingly few changes to our own day.

These cumulative diplomatic arrangements which brought West Germany and Japan into the Western alliance system were bitterly opposed by Moscow. But this was the price that the Soviet Union was forced to pay for its support (and

The tension between North and South Korea has led to clashes of varying degrees of intensity during the years since the armistice was signed. Opposite page: South Korean troops on the Han River. Above: The delegations from North Korea and the UN face each other in stony silence at the permanent talks between the UN Command Military Armistice Commission and the Communist North Korean Commission. Top: Fighting breaks out between the rival sets of border guards.

Right: In the broad sweep of history, the Korean War may well be best remembered for what did not happen rather than for what did happen, in the sense that the US decision not to resort to atomic weapons may have averted a third world war. The Korean War did, however, hasten the development of US tactical atomic weapons, one of which is shown being tested here, and the threat of the use of atomic power was used by both Truman and Eisenhower as a way of exerting pressure on the communists.

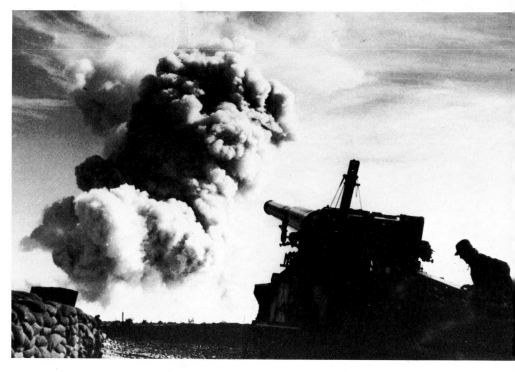

Above: The North Korean government has never ceased its propaganda campaign against what it sees as the unwarranted and baleful influence of the USA in the affairs of the South.

sponsorship) of North Korea's aggression against the ROK. Peking, too, had a major diplomatic price to pay for its intervention in Korea. For as a direct result of the Korean War, the US underwrote the continued independence of the Chinese Nationalist regime in Taiwan under Chiang Kai-shek. Because of this, Peking has not been able to make good its claim to that island.

In a more general sense, there can be little doubt that the wide-ranging measures of political, military, and economic self-defence initiated by the NATO powers as a result of the Korean War underlay the relative stability and confidence of the West during the 1950s and the 1960s.

Postscript

Yet perhaps the most important question posed by the Korean War has never been answered. Underlying the Truman–MacArthur controversy of 1951 was the question of whether the Western powers could successfully compete with the totalitarian Soviet system. President Truman believed in limiting the war in Korea. This, he maintained, would give the West time to rearm and so deter the Soviet Union and its allies from further aggression which could lead to a third world war.

General MacArthur advocated the extension of the Korean War to China with the hope of a decisive victory in the Far East and perhaps over the Soviet Union if there were a general conflict. MacArthur believed in total victory by striking at the sources of communist power. At the heart of his contention was the belief that after the early 1950s the West would lose its nuclear superiority over the East. Korea was thus the right time, by his reasoning, for a confrontation with the communist powers.

Following MacArthur's dismissal in April 1951, both parties argued their case before the famous 'MacArthur hearings' of the US Congress. The balance of the argument lay with the Truman Administration and in particular with Secretary of State Dean Acheson. He argued that the West could outpace the communist powers and that 'time is on our side if we make good use of it'.

At the time, the argument appeared persuasive. But over 30 years after the end of the Korean War, it still remains to be seen whether time is on the side of the West. Recent advances in Soviet nuclear technology, and a general process of Soviet rearmament, can support the premise that the West has not made good use of its time since the Korean War. Thus the historic question posed by that conflict remains unanswered.

Index

Figures in italics refer to captions

Acknowledgements

Photographs were supplied by Associated Press, Camera Press, Communist Party Library, C.T.K., B. N. Foliot, Robert Hunt Library, Imperial War Museum, Keystone Press Agency, Novosti Press Agency, Photri, Popperfoto, John Topham, United Nations, U.S. Air Force, U.S. Army, U.S. Army Signal Corps, U.S. Marine Corps, U.S. Navy, United Press International, U.S.I.S., Xinhua News Agency, A.D.N. Zentralbild.